ENGLISH ALFA

Berkeley, July 7/82
Elio Brachu.

Houghton Mifflin Company • Boston

Acknowledgments

Grateful acknowledgment and appreciation is made to those who helped make this edition a reality.

General Editor
Kenton Sutherland
Cañada College

Consultant
Elizabeth Bellavance
Framingham State College

Other Contributors

Jennifer Bixby
International Institute of Boston

Daphne Mackey
Boston University

Michela Larson
University of Massachusetts

Anita Reiner
University of Massachusetts

Penny Larson
Alemany Community College Center

Jack Wigfield
Alemany Community College Center

Jennifer Castello
Terry Greeley
Candy Novbakhtian

All Illustrations by Bill Ogden except page 143 by ANCO.
Cover photo by Mike Malyszko

Houghton Mifflin Company
One Beacon Street
Boston, MA 02107

ISBN 0-395-28542-9
Printed in the United States of America

Contents

Communication practice asking for information, giving information, following directions, completing sentences
Grammar What's this? It's a... — Is this a... ? Yes, it is; No, it isn't; has a... and a... — above, in, on, under — and, or

Communication practice greetings, partings, guessing what it is
Grammar What am I doing? What are you doing? What's this / that? Where's the... ? — Is this / that... ? am, are, is — have, has — am / are / is + -ing — I, you, he, she — adjectives of color and size — my, your, his, her — s for plural — a, an

Communication practice asking for information, guessing who it is, using the telephone
Grammar How old is... ? Where's...from? — am I, are you, is he / she — is he / she + -ing — this (to introduce people) — 's for possession

Communication practice giving compliments, guessing where it is, going to the post office
Grammar What color is... ? What's in / on the... ? — Commands (you) — What a... ! What a lot of... ! — Is it a... ? — this (to introduce objects) — it

Communication practice giving information, completing sentences, asking a favor
Grammar What can... ? — can, can't — adjectives as complements — behind, in front of — but

Communication practice giving information, decoding a message, unscrambling words
Grammar What's...doing? — commands (using please) — isn't + -ing — now — out, to, with

Communication practice solving word problems, spelling words, receiving gifts
Grammar How many can... ? What are these? — These are /aren't, Are they... ? Yes, they are; No, they aren't; They're... — can't you — / s / or / z / for plural — these, they

Communication practice giving information, guessing an activity, guessing where it's going
Grammar Where are... ? What are...doing? Where are...going? — Are these... ? — so, very — into, onto, out of, all over

ENGLISH ALFA

Introduction
i

1. BOOK
   BOOK

2. desk

3. pencil

4. chair

5. Pen

6. WATch

7. Rule

8. Shoe

9. Key

10. MAP

11. table

12. telephone

Tom

Betty

1.

Bicycle and Radio

2.

ball and Bird

3.

window and bed.

4.

closet and shat

5.

dog and cat

6.

coat and purse

7.

skirt   sweater

8.

Record and guitar

Introduction
iii

1. The coat is on the bed.

2. The bird is on the radio

3. The Record is on the table.

4. The purse is on the shaf.

5. The map is on the chair.

6. The guitar is in the closet

7. The key is on the purse.

8. the dog is in the car.

9. the rule is in the book

10. the pencil is under the desk

11. the book is under the table.

12. the shoe is under the bed

13. the watch is under chair.

14. the ball is under the car.

15. the cat under is the truck

(Introduction) **iii**

Introduction
iv

1	2	3	4	5	6
one	two	three	four	five	six
7	8	9	10	11	12
seven	eight	nine	ten	eleven	twelve

How many?

3　　　　　　　　　　1　　　　　　　　　　5

How many?   Use the numbers above.

1. 　　*two* 2

2. 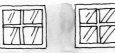　　*four*

3. 　　*six*

4. 　　*seven*

How many?   Use the vocabulary above.

■ 1. *six* (6) *six*　　　7. *one* (1)
2. *five* (5)　　　　　8. *twelve* (12)
3. *two* (2)　　　　　9. *eleven* (11)
4. *seven* (7)　　　　10. *four* (4)
5. *eight* (8)　　　　11. *two* (2)
6. *nine* (9)　　　　　12. *ten* (10)

iv (Introduction)

Introduction

V

ball   bed   book   chair
pencil   radio   shoe   table

Complete the sentences. Use the vocabulary above. *arriba*

1.

It's a _Shoe_. *shoe*

2.

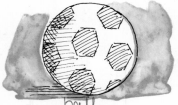

It's a _ball_.

3.

It's a _Radio_

4.

It's a _chair_

5.

It's a _pencil_

6.

It's a _book_.

7.

It's a _table_

8.

It's a _bed_.

Complete the answers.

■ 1.

What's this?
It's a purse.

3.

What's this?
It's a ___truck___

2.

Is this a bird?
___yes___ *, it is.*

4.

Is this a window?
No, ___it isn't___
___It's a table___

Answer the questions.

1.

Is this a sweater?
___yes. it is___

3.

Is this a closet?
___No. It isn't___
___it is a shaf.___

2.

Is this a pen or a pencil?
___No.___
___It's a pencil___

4.

Is this a car or a truck?
___No.___
___It's a car___

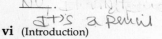

Complete and answer the questions.

■ 1.

Where's the book?
It's on the shelf.

2.

Where's the sweater?
It's _on_ the closet.

3.

Where's the shoe?
It's shoe.

4.

Where's the pen?
It is. under the chair

5.

Where's the rule?
It's under the table.

6.

Where's the radio?
It's on the shelf.   *yes   it is on the shelf*

7.

Where's the key?
It's on the purse

8.

Where's the guitar?
It's on the closet

Unit One

1•1

A. How are you?

MR. BROWN: Good morning, Mary.
MARY: Good morning, Mr. Brown.
  How are you?
MR. BROWN: Fine, thank you.
  How are you?
MARY: Fine, thank you.

Variation
BOB: Hi, my name's Bob.
  What's your name?
ANN: My name is Ann.
TED: I'm Ted.

What = que-cual
Where = donde
How = como.
this = esto (cerca)
that = eso (lejos)
Greet = saludar

B. What's this?

What's this?

    It's a pen.

   *It's a pencil.*

What's that?

    It's an orange.

   It's an apple.

Complete the sentences.

■ 1. TED: What's that?
   ANN: It's _a_ blackboard. *a*
2. TED: What's that?
   ANN: It's _a_ window.
3. TED: What's this?
   ANN: It's _a_ key.
4. TED: What's this?
   ANN: It's _a_ chair.
5. TED: What's that?
   ANN: _an_ umbrella.
6. TED: What's this?
   ANN: _a_ desk.
7. TED: What's this?
   ANN: _an_ eraser.

C. Is this a pencil?

Is this a
telephone?
Yes, it is.

Is that an eraser?
No, it isn't.
It's a key.

Complete the sentences.

■ 1. Is that an eraser? *Yes, it is.*
2. _Is_ that a pencil? *No, it isn't. It's an eraser.*
3. _Is_ that _a_ key? *Yes, It's a key.*
4. _Is_ that _a_ pen. *No, it isn't. It's a pencil.*

D. Is this your book?

Is this your book?
Yes, it is. It's my book.
No, it isn't. It's your book.

Is that my eraser?
Yes, it's your eraser.
No, it's my eraser.

Complete the sentences.

■ 1. Is this your key? *No, it isn't. It's your key.*
2. _Is_ that my eraser? *Yes, it's It's my eraser.*
3. _Is_ this your apple? *Yes, it's It's my apple.*
4. _Is_ that my book? *No, It's not book.*
No, it isn't. It's your book

$=======$ **Let's Talk** (Hablemos) $=======$

Greetings = Saludando.
Greet a new classmate.
  Hello, I'm.... What's...?   *I'm....*
  Nice to meet you. mucho gusto
(Grt) saludo
Greet a friend.
  Hi,.... Good afternoon.   *Hi.*
  How are you?   *Not bad. And you?*

1·2

A. You have a bicycle.

He has a record and a guitar. *She has* a bicycle and a car.

Complete the sentences.
- 1. You *have* a bicycle.
  2. I ___have___ record.
- 3. He ___has___ a record ___have___ a guitar.
  4. She ___has___ a bicycle ___have___ a car.

5. You ___have___ a watch.
   She ___has___ a watch and a skirt.

   WATCH. SKIRT

6. You ___have___ a dog.
   He ___has___ and a cat.

   dog CAT

7. I ___have___ a hat.
   She ___has___ a purse.

   HAT PURSE

Choose = elegir
Tell = decir
guess = adivinar

B. Colors
Complete the sentences.
- 1. The umbrella is black. It's ___a black___ umbrella. *a black*
  2. The bicycle is blue. It's ___a blue___ bicycle.
  3. The pen is brown. ___It's___ pen. *IT's a brown pen*
- 4. It's a yellow purse. It's ___yellow___. *It's yellow.*
  5. It's a red hat. ___It's___ red.
  6. It's a green pencil. It's ___green___
  7. It's a white cat. ___It's white___
  8. It's an orange book. ___It's an orange___

C. Is this a short ruler?

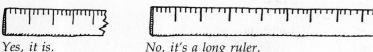

Yes, it is. *No, it's a long ruler.*

4 (four)

Is this a big radio?

Yes, it is.

No, it isn't.
It's a small radio.

Complete the sentences.

■ 1. Is this a short scarf?
   No, it's a long scarf.

2. _Is This_ big ball?
   No, it's a _Small_ *ball.*

3. _Is This_ long stick?
   No, it's a ~~short~~ stick

4. Is this a scarf or a shirt?
   No It's a shirT.

D. Where's the coat?
Where's the coat?
It's in the closet.
Where's the sweater?
It's on the floor.
Where's the shoe?
It's under the bed.

Complete the sentences.
■ 1. Where's the book?
   It's on the table.
2. Where's the coat? _____ closet. IT IN The closet.
3. Where's the radio? It's in the shelf.
4. Where's? IT ___ bed. IT is under the bed.
5. _____? _____ floor. Where's The sweater? IT's on the floor.

══ Let's Talk ══

What is it? elegir un objeto. decir donde está
Choose an object. Tell where it is.
Other students ask questions to guess the name of the object.
   It's on the... ?   Is it long?   Is it...?
   It's under the....   Is it red?

otro estudiantes hace preguntas para adivinar

the el nambee de el objeto

A. She has five birds.

1	2	3	4	5	6	7	8	9	10	11	12
one	two	three	four	five	six	seven	eight	nine	ten	eleven	twelve

One truck   Four trucks

Complete.

■ 1. You have one bird.
   I have two —. *birds*
   2. One boy — two <u>boys</u>
   3. One girl — three <u>Girls</u>
   4. One book — six <u>books</u>
   5. One coat — seven <u>coATs</u>

Make sentences. Use *have, has.*

■ 1. He, two, cat   *He has two cats.*
   2. You, eight, shoe
   3. I, nine, sweater
   4. He, ten, apple
   5. She, eleven, pencil
   6. I, twelve, record

B. His name is Mr. Brown. He's a teacher.

My name is Luis.   *Your* name is Peggy.
I am Brazilian.   *You are* English.
I'm a student.   *You're* a student.

His name is Mr. Brown.   *Her* name is Sally.
He is American.   *She is* American.
He's a teacher.   *She's* a student.

Complete the sentences.

■ 1. His name is Luis. He's Brazilian. <u>He's</u> a student. *He's*
   2. <u>Her</u> name is Peggy. She's <u>English</u> <u>SHe's</u> a student.
   3. <u>His</u> name is Mr. Brown. <u>He is</u> American. <u>He'D</u> a teacher.
   4. <u>Your</u> name is Sally. You're <u>American</u> <u>You're</u> a student.
   5. <u>My</u> name is <u>Elio</u>. I'm <u>a student.</u>

C. What's Mrs. Cooper doing?

Mr. Cooper is drinking. *He's drinking.*
Mrs. Cooper is writing. *She's writing.*
Betty Cooper is reading. *She's reading.*
Peter Cooper is cleaning. *He's cleaning.*

Complete the sentences.
■ 1. What's Mr. Cooper doing? *He's drinking coffee.*
2. What's Mrs. Cooper doing? She i___ a letter. *She's writing a letter.*
3. What's Betty doing ? _____ a book. *She's reading a book*
4. What's Peter doing ? _____ the window. *He's cleaning the window.*

D. What are you doing?
What am I doing? *I'm reading.*

Complete the sentences.
■ 1. TED: Hi, Mr. Cooper. What are you doing ? *doing*
MR. COOPER: I'm drinking coffee.
2. MARY: Hi, Mrs. Cooper. What are you doing ?
MRS. COOPER: _____ a letter. *I'm writing a letter*
3. BETTY: What am I doing? _____ a book. *You're reading a book*
4. PETER: What I doing? I'm _____ the window.
cleaning

=========== Let's Talk ===========

Partings
Say good-by to your classmates. Use one of these expressions.
Good-by, ...   *By, ...*
See you later.   *O.K.*

Grammar: Items 6, 9, 10

Review

Ask and answer questions.   Here are some examples.

What's that?   *It's a book.*
Is that a book?   *Yes, it is.*
Is that a book or an eraser?   *It's a book.*

Some alguns

Vocabulary

Nouns: floor, name, sweater   **Verbs:** are, are doing, is reading
Pronouns: I, he   **Adjectives:** big, your

Complete the sentences.   Use the vocabulary above.

1. How ____ you?   *How are you?*
2. His *Name* is Peter.
3. The ball isn't *big* .   It's small.
4. *I* have a dog and a cat.
5. What *are* you *doing*?
6. Where's the table?   *It's on the* *floor*
7. Is this my key?   *Yes, it is.   It's* *a* *key.*
8. Is that a coat or a *sweater*
9. *I* has two books.
10. Mr. Cooper *is Reading* a book.

Grammar

1. **Question word patterns**
   What's this?   What's that?
   Where's the coat?   What are you doing?
   Donde

2. What's this?   What's that?

3. **Simple present**
   I *am* (I'm) a teacher.   He *is* (He's) a student.
   You *are* (You're) Brazilian.   She *is* (She's) American.

   Is this a pen?   Yes, it *is*.
   Is that a pencil?   No, it *isn't*.   It's a pen.

   I *have* a purse.   He *has* a coat.
   You *have* a purse.   She *has* a coat.

4. **Articles**
   It's *a* ball.   It's *an* apple.

5. **Pronouns**
   I am a student.   *You* are a teacher.   *He (She)* is a teacher.

6. **Adjectives**
   What's *your* name?   *My* name's Bob.
   Her name is Sally.   *His* name is Ted.

   The ball is *brown*.   It's a *brown* ball.
   The coat is *long*.   It's a *long* coat.

7. **Conjunctions**
   He has a radio *and* a watch.
   Is this a shirt *or* a skirt?

8. **Prepositions**
   Where's the coat? It's *in* the closet.
                    It's *on* the chair.
                    It's *under* the bed.

9. **Nouns**
   One bird — two bird*s*   One shoe — two shoe*s*

10. **Present progressive**
    I'm *reading* a book.   He's *drinking* coffee.
    You're *writing* a letter.   She's *cleaning* the window.

Test • Unit 1

1•1 Complete the sentences.

1. What's your name? *My* ___NAMEis ELiO___
2. How are you? *Fine, thank* ___YOU___. *How* ___ou y___?
3. Is this a telephone? *Yes,* ___IT is___.
4. Is this an apple? *No,* ___IT isN't___
5. What's this? ___IT'S AN___ *apple.*
6. What's that? ___IT'S a___ *ruler.*

Use *a* or *an*.

7. ___aN___ orange
8. ___AN___ eraser
9. ___A___ window
10. ___AN___ umbrella
11. ___A___ chair
12. ___A___ key

/ oo

1•2 Complete the sentences.

1. The purse ___is___ white.
2. You have a dog. Mary ___has___ a dog ___and___ a cat.
3. It isn't a ___big___ shoe. It's a small shoe.
4. I ___have___ an apple. Luis ___has___ an apple and an orange.
5. The scarf ___is___ yellow.
6. Is this a long ruler? *No,* ___IT isN't___ *It's a* ___SMAIL ruler___.
7. Where's the table? *It's* ___in___ *the floor.* ___IT'S oN The floor___
8. Is this an orange ___OR___ an apple?
9. ___IT is___ *the coat? It's in the closet.* ___where is the coat?___
10. The umbrella is blue. *It's a* ___blue___ *umbrella*
11. The car is brown. *It's* ___bROWN CAR___

1•3 Complete the sentences.

1. What's Mary doing? *She's* ___reading___ *a book.*
2. What's Betty doing? *She's* ___writing___ *a letter.*
3. Her name is Sally. ___She's___ *a student.*
4. Your name is Mr. Brown. ___He's___ *a teacher.*
5. Mr. Cooper is drinking coffee. ___He's___ *drinking coffee.*
6. Hello, Peter! What are you doing? ___He's___ *cleaning the window.*
7. ___Your___ *name is Luis.* He's Brazilian.
8. This is Peter's mother. ___Her___ *name is Mrs. Cooper.*
9. This is Peter's father. ___He___ *name is Mr. Cooper.*
10. One apple — two ___Apples___
11. One car — six ___CARS___

/ oo

Maintaining Skills

1•1 Complete the sentences.

1. _Good_ morning. How _are_ you?
2. TED: Hi, _My_ name is Ted. What's your name?
3. ANN: _Hi_! How are you?
4. Is this your pencil? No, _it isn't your pencil_
5. Is that my orange? Yes, _it's_. _your orange_
6. What's this? _It is a_ blackboard.
7. What's that? _It's a_ window.
8. _What's_ this? _It's an_ eraser.
9. _What's_ that? _It's an_ umbrella.
10. _Is_ that your book? Yes, it's _my_ book.
11. _Is_ this my key? No, it's _my_ key.
12. It's _your_ eraser.

1•2 Complete the sentences.

1. _Where's_ the sweater? _It's_ on the floor.
2. I _have_ a record.
3. The ball is brown. _It's_ brown ball.
4. You _have_ a radio.
5. She _has_ a radio _and_ an umbrella.
6. Is this a book _and_ a ball?
7. The car is blue. It's a _blue_
8. It's a yellow hat. _It's_ yellow.
9. The coat _is_ red.
10. Is this a big shoe? No, it's a _small_ shoe.   / 00
11. Where's the shoe? It's _under_ the floor.

1•3 Complete the sentences.

1. five, _six_, _seven_, eight, _nine_, _ten_, eleven
2. His name _is_ Peter. _He's_ American.
3. My name is Sally. I'm American. _I'm_ a student.
4. He's _cleaning_ the window.
5. She's _reading_ a book.   / 00
6. I'm _writing_ a letter.
7. He's _drinking_ coffee.
8. He has _nine_ (9) trucks.
9. one boy — two _boys_
10. eight dogs — one _dog_
11. one closet — two _closets_

Unit Two

A. This is the Cooper family.

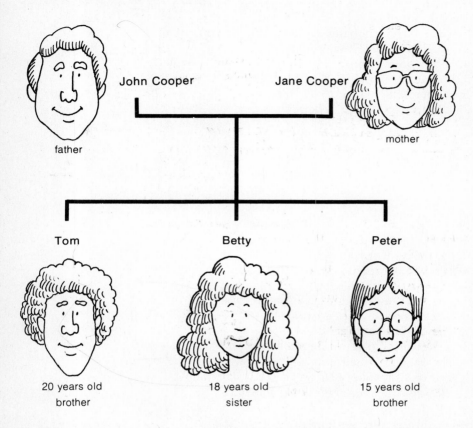

John Cooper   Jane Cooper

father

mother

Tom   Betty   Peter

20 years old
brother

18 years old
sister

15 years old
brother

Mrs. Jane Cooper is Peter's mother. She's Betty's mother, too. She's Tom's mother, too. Mr. John Cooper is Tom's father. He's Betty's father, too. He's Peter's father, too. Tom Cooper is Betty's brother. He's Peter's brother, too. Peter Cooper is Tom's brother. He's Betty's brother, too.

Look at the pictures and complete the sentences.
■ 1. Peter: He's Betty's brother. He's Tom's brother, too.
　2. Betty: She's Tom's _sister_ She's _Peter's_ sister, too.
　3. Tom: He's Peter's _Brother._ He's _Betty's_ too. _Betty's brother, too._
　4. Mr. Cooper: He's Peter _father._ He's Betty's father, _too_.
　5. Mrs. Cooper: She's Tom's _mother._ _She's_ Peter's mother, too.
　6. Mr. Cooper is Peter's father. He's Betty's _father_, too.

B. Is he Peter's father?

Alan Crane is Tom's friend. Is Mr. Cooper Alan's father? *No, he isn't.*

Complete the questions.   Answer *Yes, he is* **(1) or** *No, he isn't* **(2).**

■ 1. Is Mr. Cooper Tom's father? *Yes, he is.*
   Is he Peter's brother? *No, he isn't.*
   Is he Peter's father? *Yes, he is.*

  2. Is Tom Peter's brother? yes, he is
   _Is_ he Betty's brother? yes, she is
   _Is he_ Alan's brother? No, she isn't

  3. Is Alan Mr. Cooper's friend? No, he isn't
   _Is he_ Tom's father? No, he isn't
   _Is he_ Betty's father? No, He isn't

  4. _Is_ Peter Betty's brother? yes, He
   _Is He_ Betty's father? No, she isn't

C. Is she Betty's mother?

Helen is Betty's friend.   Mrs. Cooper is Betty's mother.
Is she Helen's mother? *No, she isn't.*

Complete and answer the questions.

■ 1. Is Mrs. Cooper Betty's mother? *Yes, she is.*
   Is she Helen's mother? *No, she isn't.*

  2. _Is_ Helen Peter's sister? No, she isn't
   Is she Tom's sister?   No, she isn't

  3. _Is_ Mrs. Cooper Peter's mother? yes, she is
   Is she Tom's mother? yes, she is

  4. _Is_ Betty Helen's friend? yes, she is
   Is she Tom's sister? yes, she is
   Is she Peter's sister? yes, she is

  5. _Is_ Helen Betty's friend? yes, she is
   Is she Tom's sister? No, she isn't

=============== Let's Talk ===============

What's your friend's name?

Ask your classmate these questions.
   What's your father's name?   *His name is* ..Humberto
   What's your mother's name?   *Her.* Name is MARIA
   What's your brother's name?   His NAme is Humberto
   What's your sister's name?   Hee name is Luisa
   What's your friend's name?   His NAme is Roberto

Consequir
Draw your family tree.

Mar
Grammar: Items 1 and 4

cual es nombre de un amigo

A. This is Betty's friend. Her name is Helen.

BETTY: Hello, my name is Betty.
  What's your name?
ROGER: My name is Roger.
  What's his name?
BETTY: His name is Luis.
ROGER: What's her name?
BETTY: Her name is Helen.

Complete the sentences.
■ 1. This is Peter's brother. _His_ name is Tom.   *His*
 2. This is Betty's friend. _Her_ name is Helen.
 3. This is Betty's father. _His_ name is John Cooper.
 4. This is Helen's mother. _Her_ name is Mrs. Wilson.
 5. _This is_ Peter's mother. _Her Name_ is Jane Cooper.
 6. _this is_ Betty's brother. His name _is_ Tom.
 7. _this is_ Tom's friend. His _name_ is Roger Smith.
 8. _this is_ Peter's sister. _Her_ name is Betty.
 9. _this is_ Betty's mother. _Her__ is Mrs. Cooper. _Her Name is Mrs Cooper_
 10. _this is_ Helen's friend. His _name is_ Luis. _His Name is Luis_

B. Are you Chinese?

Are you Chinese? *No, I'm not.*
Are you Spanish? *Yes, I am. I'm Spanish. I'm not Chinese.*

Complete and answer the questions.
■ 1. Are you American? *Am I American? Yes, I am.*
■ 2. Are you Spanish? *Am I Spanish? No, I'm not.*
 3. _Are_ you Chinese? _Am I chinese? No, I'm Not_
 4. _Are you_ Canadian? _Am I canadian? No I'm Not_

C. How old is Peter? Where is he from?

13	14	15	16	17	18	19	20
thirteen	fourteen	fifteen	sixteen	seventeen	eighteen	nineteen	twenty

Peter is fifteen years old. He's from Chicago. He's American. Elena is nineteen years old. She's from Bogotá. She's Colombian.

Complete the sentences.

■ 1. How old is Mark? *Mark is sixteen.*
    Where is he from? *He's from Boston. He's American.*
 2. How old is Tom? *Tom is* twenty (20) years old
    Where is he from? *He's* from *Chicago.*
    He's *American.*
 3. How old is Helen? *Helen is* seventeen (17). seventeen years old
    Where she from? *She's* from *Toronto.*
    She's *Canadian.*
 4. How old Paolo? *Paolo is* fourteen (14). fourteen years old
    Where's he from? *He's* from *Rio de Janeiro.*
    What's he's *Brazilian.*

D. How old are you?

MR. BROWN: How old are you, Peter?
PETER: I'm fifteen years old.
MR. BROWN: How old is Helen? Is she fifteen, too?
PETER: No, she isn't. She's seventeen.

Variation

MR. BROWN:	PETER:
How old are you, Peter?	*I'm fifteen.*
Is Helen fifteen, too?	*No, she's seventeen.*

Complete and answer the questions.

■ 1. How old are you, Elena? *I'm nineteen.*
 2. How old are you, Betty? I'm *eighteen.*
 3. How old is Peter? He's *fifteen.*
 4. How old is Betty? *She's* eighteen
 5. Is she eighteen? Yes, she is
 6. Is Peter seventeen (17)? No, he isn't
 7. Is he twelve (12)? No, he's fifteen years old.
 8. How old are you, Peter? I'm *fifteen years old.*

Are = A
How = H
old = O
Is = I

───────────────── *Let's Talk* ─────────────────

Who is it?

Choose a famous person from another country.
Other students ask questions to guess who the person is.
    Is it a man or a woman?   *It's a . . . .*
    Is he (she) American?
    How old?
    Is . . . ?

A. Really?

ROGER:	HELEN:
Hi.	*Hello.*
My name's Roger. What's your name?	*Helen Wilson.*
Are you Canadian?	*Yes, I am.*
Are you from Montreal?	*No, I'm from Toronto.*
Really? How old are you?	*Seventeen. And you?*
I'm nineteen.	

Complete and answer the questions.

■ 1. Are you from Chicago? *No, I'm not. I'm from.* Venezuela
2. Are you from Paris? NO, I'M NOT. I'm from venezuela
3. Are you Hong Kong? NO I'm NOT. I'M from venezuela
4. Are you F Nairobi? NO, I'm NOT. I'm from Venezuela
5. Are you F New York? NO, I'M NOT. I'm from Venezuela

B. The English alphabet.

E h · gi eit gi ker el em en

| Aa — Bb — Cc — Dd — Ee — Ff — Gg — Hh — Ii — Jj — Kk — Ll — Mm — Nn — Oo |
| Pp — Qq — Rr — Ss — Tt — Uu — Vv — Ww — Xx — Yy — Zz zi |

qiu ar uay

Spell the words.

1. Afternoon   2. Morning   3. Thanks   4. Your name

PAteando

C. Is she writing?

Is Tom kicking the ball?
Yes, he is.
Is he reading a book?
No, he isn't.
He's playing soccer.

Complete and answer the questions.

■ 1. Is Mrs. Cooper sitting? *Yes, she is. She's sitting.*
  2. _IS_ Betty running? *No, she isn't she's writing.*
  3. _IS_ Peter sitting? *No, the isn't He's standing.*
  4. _IS_ Mr. Cooper ~~playing~~ soccer? *No, he isn't He's coffee.* He's drinking a cup coffee

D. Welcome to Chicago!

HELEN: Is Tom your brother, Betty?
BETTY: Yes, he is.
HELEN: Oh? How old is he?
BETTY: He's twenty.
HELEN: No, he isn't!
BETTY: Yes, he is!
PETER: Hey, Tom! Come here!
TOM: What?
PETER: How old are you?
TOM: I'm twenty.
BETTY: Tom, this is Helen.
TOM: Hi, Helen!
  Where are you from?
HELEN: Hello, Tom.
  I'm from Toronto.
  I'm Canadian.
TOM: Welcome to Chicago!
HELEN: Thank you, Tom.

Answer the questions.

■ 1. Is Betty Tom's sister? *Yes, she is.*
  2. Is Tom Betty's brother? Yes, He is
  3. Is Helen Betty's sister? No, she isn't
  4. Is Tom twenty years old? yes, He is twenty.
  5. Where is Helen from? She is from toronto, He's CANADIAN.
  6. Is Helen Spanish? No, she isn't
  7. Where is Peter from? He is from chicago. He is American.
  8. How old is Tom? He's twenty years old.
    (Hav)

═══════════════ *Let's Talk* ═══════════════

The telephone

Call Information. Another student or your teacher is the operator.
Ask for the number of a friend.

Hello.   *The number for Ed P. Cox please.*
How do you spell it?   *C — O — X*
What are his initials again?   *E and P*
The number is.... 8487176   *Thank you.*
You're welcome.

inicial

Review

Ask and answer questions. Here are some examples.

What's Betty doing? *She's reading.*

Is she standing? *No, she isn't.*

Vocabulary

Nouns: brother, father, friend, mother, sister
Verbs: is sitting
Adverbs: here
Prepositions: from
Expressions: How old are you, Welcome to

Complete the sentences. Use the vocabulary above.

1. Betty is Tom's *sister*
2. Peter is Betty's *Brother*
3. Helen is Betty's *friend*
4. Mrs. Cooper is Betty's *mother*
5. Luis is *from* Brazil.
6. Mr. Cooper is Tom's *father*
7. Come *here*, Tom.
8. *is sitting*, Tom? — *How old are you tom?*
9. She isn't standing. She's *sitting*
10. *Welcome to* Mexico.

18 (eighteen)

Grammar

1. **Simple present**
   Are you fifteen? *Am* I fifteen? Yes, I *am*.
   Is she Betty's mother? Yes, she *is*.
   Is he Tom's father? No, he *isn't*.

   He *is* Betty's brother.
   He's Betty's brother.

2. **Pronouns**
   This is Mr. Cooper.
   This is Mrs. Cooper.

3. **Nouns**
   Mrs. Cooper is Betty's mother.
   Mr. Cooper is Tom's father.

4. **Adjectives**
   Hello, *my* name is Betty. *His* name is Luis.
   Her name is Helen. What's *your* name?

5. **Question word patterns**
   How old are you?
   Where are you from?

6. **Present progressive**
   Is Tom *kicking* the ball? Yes, he is.
   Is she *writing*? No, she isn't.

Test • Unit 2

2•1 Complete the sentences. Use *he's* or *she's*.

1. This is Tom. _He's_ Betty's brother.
2. This is Betty. _DHe's_ Tom's sister.
3. This is Mr. Cooper. _He's_ Tom's father.
4. This is Mrs. Cooper. _She's_ Tom's mother.
5. This is Peter. _He's_ Tom's brother.

Complete the sentences.

6. _Is_ Tom Betty's father? *No, he* _isn't_.
7. _Is_ Betty Tom's sister? *Yes,* _she is_.
8. _Is_ Helen Betty's sister? *No,* _she isn't_.
9. _Is_ Peter Betty's brother? *Yes,* _he is_.
10. _Is_ Mrs. Cooper Betty's mother? *Yes,* _she is_.

2•2 Complete the sentences.

1. This is Peter's brother. _His_ name is Tom.
2. This is Peter's sister. _Her_ name is Betty.
3. Mary is American. She's _from_ America.
4. Are _you_ American?
5. Is Ann Chinese? *No,* _she_ isn't.
6. Bob _is_ seventeen. He's _from_ New York City.
7. _Is_ she sixteen? *Yes,* _she is_.
8. How old _are_ you? _I'm_ *twenty years old.*
9. How old _is_ he? _He's_ *seventeen* _years old_.
10. How old _is_ Betty? _She is_ *eighteen.*

2•3 Complete the sentences.

1. _Are_ you _from_ Boston?
2. Elena is Colombian. _She is from_ Bogotá. _She is from_
3. Is Tom _kicking_ the ball?
   Yes, _He's_ playing soccer. _(Is he kicking...)_
4. _Is_ Mrs. Cooper _drinking_ coffee?
   No, _she is_ reading a book. _No, she isn't._
is she 5. _Standing_ or is she sitting? *She's standing.*
_is he_ 6. _cleaning_ the bicycle or the car? *He's cleaning the car.*
7. Are you from Spain? _Am_ *I from Spain? No, I'm not.*
8. Hi, Helen. _Where's_ from? _Hi, Helen where are you from_
9. _My_ name's Elena. I'm _from_ Bogotá.
10. _____ a letter or a book? *She's writing a book.*
Is she writing

Please Make Corrections!

1•1 Complete the sentences.

1. Hi, my _Name's_ Bob.
2. Hello, Ted. _How Are_ you?
3. Fine, _thanks_.
4. _What's_ this? *It's an apple.*
5. What's that? _It's A_ *key.*
6. Is this your pencil? *Yes,* _It is_.
7. Is that your umbrella? *No,* _it isn't_ ← *No, it isn't*
8. Good-by, Ted. _See you_ tomorrow.
9. _Is_ that a window?
10. _Is_ this a telephone?

please correct this.

1•2 Complete the sentences.

1. You _have_ a wristwatch.
2. Mary _has_ a bicycle.
3. Peter has a car _and_ a bicycle.
4. The car _is_ red.
5. _It's_ red car. ← *It's a red car.*
6. Is this a _short_ ruler? *No, it's a long ruler.*
7. _Is_ this a _small_ shoe? *No, it's a big shoe.*
8. _Where's_ the sweater? *It's on the chair.*
9. Is the coat under the bed? *No, it's* _on_ *the closet.*
10. _Is_ this a table or a chair?
11. Where's the shoe? *It's* _on_ *the floor.*

Please correct this.

1•3 Complete the sentences.

1. One, _two_, _three_, four.
2. _seven_, eight, nine, _ten_.
3. My _name_ is Luis. _I'm from_ Brazilian.
4. Your name _is_ Sally. _you are_ American.
5. Her name is Sally. _She is_ a student.
6. Peter _is cleaning_ the window.
7. Mr. Cooper _is drinking_ coffee.
8. What are _you_ doing? _I'm_ *reading a book.*
9. What's Peter _doing_?
10. This is Peter's mother. _Her_ name is Mrs. Cooper.
11. This is Peter's father. _His_ name is Mr. Cooper.

1 00

Unit Three

3·1

A. What's this? What's that?

What's this?
It's a letter.

What's that?
It's a box.

Complete the sentences.

■ 1. What's this? *It's a bench.*

■ 2. What's that? *It's an airplane.*

3. It's __an__ island.   *airland*

4. It's __a__ tree.

■ 1. Is this a bicycle?
   No, it isn't.   *narcot*
   It's a motorcycle.

2. Is that __an__ apple?
   No, _ITSN'T_. _IT's a_ banana.

3. Is this __a__ chair?
   No, _ITSN'T_. _IT's a_ sofa.

4. Is that __a__ tree?
   NO, ITSN'T. _IT's a_ bush.

22 (twenty-two)

B. It's on the floor.

Look at the record
It's on the record player.

Look at the orange.
It's in the bowl. *bowl*

Look at Peter's room.   Complete the sentences.
■ 1. Look at the guitar. It's _ON_ the floor. *on*
2. Look at the sweater. _IT'S ON_ the chair.
3. _Look At_ the record. _IT'S ON the_ record player.
4. _Look At The_ coat. _____. _IT'S IN the closet._
5. _Look At The_ letter. _____. _IT'S ON The table._

ON = ENCIMA
IN = DENTRO

closet

C. It's in the book.

Is the pencil in the book or on the table? *It's in the book.*

Complete and answer the questions.
■ 1. Is the record player on the chair or on the table?
   It's on the table.
2. Is the coat _IN_ the closet or on the chair?
   It's _IN The closet_
3. Is the book on the chair or _ON_ the table?
   It's _ON the table._

Let's Talk

Where is it?

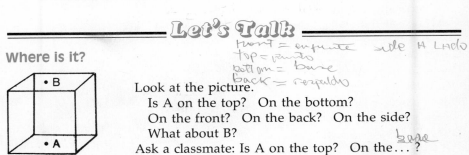

front = enfrente   side A LADO
top = punto
bottom = base
back = respaldo

Look at the picture.
Is A on the top? On the bottom?
On the front? On the back? On the side?
What about B?
Ask a classmate: Is A on the top? On the... ? *base*

3•2

A. What's on the wall?

BILL: What's on the wall?
   Is it a map?
BETH: No, it isn't.
   It's a poster.

Complete the sentences.

■ 1. BILL: What's in the yard? Is it a stick?
   BETH: No, it isn't. It's a ruler.
2. BILL: What's on the bench? Is it a ball?
   BETH: No, _isn't_. _It's_ an apple.
3. BETH: _What's in_ the tree? Is it a bird?
   BILL: No, _it isn't_. _It's_ a kite. _Sait_

YARD = patio
STICK = palo.
kite = cometa,
     papagayo.

B. What color is it?

Look at the apple. What color is it? It's.. _green_

Complete and answer the questions.

■ 1. Look at your book. What color is it? _It is green and black_
2. Look at your chair. _What_ color is it? _it's green_
3. Look at the floor. _What color_ is it? _it's green._
4. Look at the wall. _____? _What color is it? It's beige._

C. It's big.

This is Elena. She's
   Colombian. She's nineteen.
This is Roger. He's
   Tom's friend. He's nineteen.
This is an apple.
   It's big. It's _a big apple_

Complete the sentences.
■ 1. This is an airplane. _It's_ big. *It's*
  2. This is Mary. _She's_ American.
  3. This is Peter. _He's_ fifteen.
  4. This is an apple. _It's_ green.
  5. This is Betty. _She's_ Peter's sister.
  6. This is a shoe. _It's_ black.
  7. This is Mr. Cooper. _He's_ Peter's father.
  8. This is Elena. _She's_ nineteen.
  9. This is Roger. _He's_ Tom's friend.
  10. This is a book. _It's_ long.

D. What a lot of records!

ELENA: Helen, look at my records.
HELEN: What a lot of records!
  And what a nice record player!

PETER: Hey, Dad. Look at my new coat!
MR. COOPER: What a nice coat, Peter!

Complete the sentences.
■ 1. LUIS: Peter, is this your shoe?
    PETER: No, it _isn't_. *isn't*
    _It's_ Tom's shoe.
    LUIS: _What a_ big shoe!
  2. JANE COOPER: Is the dog in the yard?
    JOHN COOPER: No, _it isn't._
    _It's_ on my chair.
    JANE: _What a_ bad _dog_!
  3. BETTY: Is this your picture, Tom?
    TOM: Yes, _it_ is.
    _It's_ my picture.
    BETTY: _What a_ nice _picture_
  4. MRS. COOPER: Is this your book?
    LUIS: No, _it_ isn't.
    _It's_ Roger's _book_
    MRS. COOPER: _What a_ big _book_!

Let's Talk

Compliments Say something nice about a person.
Show your classmate something.
  This is my . . . .   *What a nice . . . .*
  This is . . . .   *What a . . . .*
  Look at my . . . .

Grammar: Items 1, 3, 8   (twenty-five) **25**

A. That's right.

PETER: Hi, Betty! Hi, Elena!
BETTY: Hi. What's that,
 Peter. Is it your bicycle?
PETER: No, it isn't.
 It's my motorcycle.
ELENA: Your motorcycle?
PETER: That's right. It's
 my motorcycle. I'm cleaning it.
ELENA: What a dirty
 motorcycle!

Complete and answer the questions.

■ 1. Is Peter in the yard? *Yes, he is.*
 2. What is Peter doing? _____ *his motorcycle.*
 3. Is Elena Betty's friend or her sister?
 4. Is Elena Peter's sister? *No,*
 5. Is Peter Betty's brother?
 6. Is the motorcycle in the yard or on the floor?

B. What a big family!

ALAN: Peter, this is my family.
PETER: What a lot of brothers and sisters!
ALAN: Chris is on the floor.
PETER: Is Chris a boy or a girl?
ALAN: Chris is a boy. He's three years old.
 Ann is talking on the telephone.
PETER: How old is she?
ALAN: She's fifteen.
PETER: And on the sofa?
ALAN: That's Ted and Alice and Carol. Ted's eleven.
 Alice is eight and Carol is six.
PETER: What a big family!

Complete and answer the questions.

■ 1. Is Peter Alan's friend? *Yes, he is.*
2. Is Chris in the closet? *No, he* _isn't_. *He's* _on_ _the floor_
3. Is Chris a girl? *No,* _He's_ *a boy.*
4. How old is Ann? _She's fifteen_
5. Is Ted in the chair? _~~He's in it~~ No, he is on The sofa._
6. How old is Ted? _He's eleven_
7. Is Carol Alan's mother? _No, she isn't_
8. Is Alice eight? _yes, she is_
9. Is Ted Peter's brother? _No, he isn't._
10. How old is Carol? _She's six_
11. Is Chris Ted's brother? _yes, he is_
12. What is Ann doing? _She is Talking on telephone_
13. Is Ted on the sofa? _yes, he is_

C. Are you Spanish?

TOM: Hello, Elena.
ELENA: Hi, Tom. How are you?
TOM: Fine, thanks. Elena, this is my friend, Luis.
   He's in your English class.
ELENA: That's right. Hi, Luis.
   Are you Spanish?
LUIS: No, I'm Brazilian. Are you Spanish?
ELENA: No, I'm Colombian. Welcome to Chicago, Luis.
LUIS: Thanks, Elena. See you in English class.
ELENA: Yes, see you later.
TOM: Good-by.

Complete the sentences.

■ 1. Elena is _tom's_ friend. *Tom's*
2. Luis is Tom's _friend_
3. Luis is _Brazilian_ He's _from_ Brazil.
4. Elena _isn't_ Spanish. _She's_ Colombian.
5. Luis is _in_ Elena's English class.
6. _Tom_ isn't in the English class.

Let's Talk

The post office

Talk to a clerk in the post office (another student).
Mail one of these gifts: a book, an umbrella, a shirt.

Yes?	*Air mail postage, please.*
Is it a book?	*No, it isn't. It's a.. _Shirt_*
O.K. Where to?	*To... . _Japan_*
To... ?	*That's right.*
O.K.	

(twenty-seven) **27**

Review

Ask and answer questions.   Here are some examples:

Where's the radio?   *It's on the shelf.*

Look at the . . . .

What a . . . .

What a lot of . . . !

Vocabulary

Nouns: bowl, class, record player, wall

Verbs: look

Adjectives: bad, right

Prepositions: in

Expressions: what a, what a lot of

Complete the sentences.   Use the vocabulary above.

1. _____ oranges!
2. _____ dirty motorcycle.
3. The dog is on the table.   What a ___ dog!
4. The picture is on the _____
5. That's _____
6. The apples are in the _____ .
7. The cat is _____ the box.
8. The record is on the _____
9. _____ at the nice car.
10. He's in my English _____

Grammar

1. **Question word patterns**
   What's this?   What's that?
   What's on the wall?   What color is it?

2. **Articles**
   It's *a* car.   It's *an* airplane.

3. **Present tense**
   Is this a bowl?   *Is* that a box?
   Yes, it is.   Yes, it is.

   Is it a banana?   *Are* you Spanish?
   No, it isn't. It's an orange. *Am* I Spanish? Yes, I am.

4. **Commands**
   Look at the blackboard.   Look at the wall.

5. **Prepositions**
   Look *at* the bush.   It's *in* the yard.
   Look *at* the record.   It's *on* the record player.

6. **Conjunctions**
   Is the kite in the tree *or* on the bench?   It's in the tree.

   Papagallo
7. **Pronouns**
   This is an island.   *This* is a sofa.

he	she	it
Peter Mr. Cooper	Betty Mrs. Cooper Ann	a radio an umbrella a record player

8. **Exclamations**
   What a big family!
   What a lot of brothers and sisters!
   What a lot of coffee!

9. **Nouns**
   Is Peter Alan's friend?   yes, he is

3•1 Complete the sentences.

1. _What's_ this? *It's a record player.*
2. What's on the record player? _It's_ a record.
3. Is the apple on the desk _or_ on the floor?
4. Peter's coat is _in_ the closet.
5. What's _this_? *It's a bowl.*
6. This _is_ a guitar. It's _on_ the floor.
7. _Is_ this a bench? *No, it isn't.*
8. _Is_ that a bush? *No, it isn't. It's a tree.*
9. Is the banana in the box or in the bowl? _It's in_ *the bowl.*
10. _Look_ at the apple. *It's red.*
11. Look _at_ the record. It's _on_ the record player.

3•2 Complete the sentences.

1. This is Mrs. Cooper. _She's_ Tom's mother.
2. _What a_ nice bicycle, Roger!
3. Mr. Cooper is Tom's father. _He's_ Peter's father, too.
4. _What's_ on the table? _Is it_ a radio?
5. This is my friend Elena. _She's_ Colombian.
6. What _color_ is the scarf? _It's_ *blue and red.*
7. This is Luis. _He's_ Tom's friend.
8. He has three cars. _____ of cars! *What a lot of cars!*
9. She has a new coat. _What a_ nice coat!
10. _This is_ an airplane. *It's big.*

3•3 Complete the sentences.

1. Is Alan Tom's brother? *No,* _he isn't._ _He's_ *Tom's friend.*
2. Is that your car? _That's_ *right. It's my car.*
3. _How old_ Ann? *She's fifteen.* (How old is Ann?)
4. Chris is _on_ the sofa.
5. Elena, _will_ you Italian? *No,* _I'm_ *Colombian.*
6. Welcome _to_ Chicago.
7. What's Ann doing? *She's* _talking on_ *the telephone.*
8. Is that your motorcycle? _That's_ *right.* _It's_ *my motorcycle.*
9. _Is_ Chris Ted's brother? *Yes,* _he is._
10. Is Chris a boy _or_ a girl? *He's* _boy._ (He's a boy.)

Maintaining Skills

2•1 Complete the sentences. Use *mother, father, sister, brother*.

1. Mrs. Cooper is Peter's _Mother_.
2. Mr. Cooper is Betty's _father_.
3. Tom is Betty's _brother_.
4. Betty is Tom's _sister_.
5. Betty is Peter's _sister_, too.

Complete the sentences. Use *she's* and *he's*.

6. _She's_ Peter's mother.
7. _he's_ Tom's father.
8. _She's_ Tom's sister.
9. _He's_ Peter's brother.

Answer the questions.

10. Is Tom Peter's brother? _yes, He is_
11. Is Betty Tom's sister? _yes, she is_
12. Is Mrs. Cooper Peter's father? _No, she isn't._

2•2 Complete the sentences.

1. My name is Betty. What's _your_ name?
2. This is Tom's sister. _Her_ name is Betty. (Her)
3. This is Tom's father. _His_ name is Mr. Cooper. (His)
4. How old _are_ you? _I'm_ fifteen.
5. How old _is_ she? _She's_ thirteen.

2•3 Complete the sentences.

1. How _old_ is he? *He's* _twenty_ (20).
2. Where _is_ she from? *She's* _from_ *Canada*.
3. Is Betty Cooper American? _yes, she isn't_
4. Helen _is_ sitting. _is_ she _writing_ a book? (is she reading)
5. Mr. Cooper _is_ standing. _is_ he _drinking_ coffee?

Extra!

His name is Tom. His family's name is Cooper. He's American. He's from Chicago. He's a student. He's twenty years old. He's studying French.

Who are you?
My name is.... My family's name is.... I'm....

(thirty-one) **31**

Unit Four

4·1

A. Can you see Peter?   Yes, I can.

BETTY: Look, Helen. What can you see in my picture?

HELEN: I can see a lake and a house.

BETTY: Can you see a tree?

HELEN: Yes, I can. I can see a bird, too.

BETTY: Can you see Peter?

HELEN: No, I can't.

BETTY: Yes, you can see Peter. Look under the tree.

HELEN: Oh, yes. I can see Peter under the tree.

See = Ver
but = Pero

Complete and answer the questions.

■ 1. Can you see Peter? *Yes, I can.*
2. CAN you see a house? *Yes, I* CAN
3. CAN you SEE a lake? *Yes,* I CAN
4. CAN bird? *Yes, I can.*
CAN YOU SEE A

B. No, he can't.

Can Peter see a house? *No, he can't.*

Complete and answer the questions.

■ 1. Can Peter see a dog? *No, he can't.*
2. CAN Peter see a ball? *No, he* CAN'T
3. CAN Peter SEE Helen? *No,* HE CAN'T
CAN he SEE Betty? *No, he can't.*

C. Helen can see a lake.   She can't see a cat.

What can Helen see? *She can see a lake.*

What can't Helen see? *She can't see a cat.*

32 (thirty-two)

Complete the sentences and answer the questions.

■ 1. Helen can see a tree. She _CAN'T_ see a table. *can't*

2. Helen _CAN_ see a lake. She _CAN'T_ see a cat.

3. Helen _CAN see_ Peter. She _____ Tom. *She can't see Tom.*

4. She _____ bird. _____ ball. *She can see a bird. She can't see a ball.*

■ 5. Can Betty see a house and a lake? *Yes, she can.*

6. _CAN_ Helen _see_ Peter and a mouse? *Yes, she* _CAN_.

7. _CAN_ you _see_ Helen and Betty? *NO, you CAN'T*

8. _CAN_ Peter _see_ Helen and Betty? *NO, he CAN'T*

D. I can see a man, but I can't see a woman.

What can you see? *I can see a man.*
What can't you see? *I can't see a woman.*

Can you see a man and a woman?
I can see a man, but I can't see a woman.
I can't see a woman, but I can see a man.

Complete and answer the questions.

■ 1. Can you see a boy and a girl?
I can see a girl, but I can't see a boy.
I can't see a boy, but I can see a girl.

2. Can you see a lamp and a chair?
I _CAN see a_ lamp, but I _CAN'T. See a chair_
I _can't see a_ chair, but I _can see a lamp._

3. Can you see a cage and a box?
I can see ___ a cage _____ box, but I can't see a box
I can't see a box _____ cage.
but I can see a cage.

─────── *Let's Talk* ───────

What can you do?

What are three things you can do? What are three things you can't do?
Ask a classmate questions.
Can you...?

Tell the class what you can do.
I can..., but...can't.   We can..., but we can't....

Grammar: Items 1, 2   (thirty-three) **33**

A. Peter is behind Betty.
Mrs. Cooper is in front of Tom.
Mr. Cooper is behind Tom.

Complete the sentences.
■ 1. Mrs. Cooper is *behind* Peter.
  Peter is *in front of* Mrs. Cooper.
2. Peter is _behind_ Betty.
  Betty is _in front of_ Peter.
3. Tom is _behind_ Mrs. Cooper.
  Tom is _in front of_ Mr. Cooper.

beside = a lado
behind = detras

B. What can you see in Tom's room?

be

Cartain
Cortina

Complete and answer the questions.
■ 1. What can you see in Tom's room? *I can see a bookcase.* biblioteca
2. _What_ can you see on the wall? I ____ a poster. I can see a poster
3. _What can you see_ on the table? I _can see_ TV.
4. _What can_ you _see_ under the bed? I can see a mouse, but I can see a shoe, too.
5. _Can you_ in front of the bookcase? I can see basket.
6. ____ behind the basket? I can see a cat bicase
  can you see   I can see a cat and a Bookcase

C. Where's the curtain?
Vocabulary:
  curtain, window
Make a question:
  Where's the curtain?   *Where is the window.*
Answer the question:
  It's in front of the window.

Make and answer questions.   Look at Tom's room.
■ 1. cat, basket   Where's the cat? *It's behind the basket.*
  2. lamp, table   *Where's* the lamp? *It's on the table.*
  3. basket, bookcase *Where's the basket? It is in front of bookcase*
  4. mouse, bed   *Where's the mouse? It's under the bed.*
  5. sweater, chair *Where's the sweater? It's on the chair.*

D. Is the mouse under the bed or on the bed?
Vocabulary:
  mouse, under / on, bed
Question:
  Is the shoe under the bed or on the bed?
Answer:
  It's under the bed.

Make and answer the questions about Tom's room.
■ 1. basket, in front of / behind, bookcase
     Is the basket in front of the bookcase or behind the bookcase?
     It's in front of the bookcase.
  2. lamp, under / on, table
     Is ____?   *Is the lamp on the table or under the table?*
     It's *on the table.*
  3. curtain, in front of / in, window
     Is ____? *Is the curtain in front of the window or in the window?*
     It's *in front of the window.*
  4. cat, in front of / behind, basket
     Is ____? *Is the cat in front of the basket or behind the basket.*
     It's *behind the basket.*

═══════════════ Let's Talk ═══════════════

Can you help me?
Ask a classmate to do you a favor.
   Can you help?   *Sure.*
   Can you do my homework?   *No.*
   Can you... ?   *Sure.*
   Thanks a lot.

A. Where's the bird?

MRS. COOPER: Hey, the cage is open!
  Where's the bird?
BETTY: Is it under the table?
TOM: No, it isn't.
PETER: Mother, is it behind the door?
MRS. COOPER: No, it isn't. The door
  is shut. I can see the cat, but I
  can't see the bird.
BETTY: Oh — oh! The window is open.
  Tom, can you see the
  bird in the yard?
TOM: No, I can't. Is it behind the curtain?
BETTY: No, it isn't.
TOM: Peter, can you see the bird
  under the bed?
PETER: No, I can't.
MRS. COOPER: Aha! I can see the bird!
BETTY: Where?
MRS. COOPER: In your shoe!
BETTY: In my shoe? Where?
MRS. COOPER: Under the chair.

shut = cerrar

Complete the sentences and answer the questions.

■ 1. Hey, the cage is _open_! *open*
  2. Tom, can _you see_ the bird _in_ the yard?
  3. The window _is_ open.
  4. The door is _shut_.
  5. Is the bird behind the curtain?
    No, _it isn't_   *I can't see*
  6. I can see the cat, but _____ the bird.
  7. _can_ you _see_ the bird under the bed?
    No, _I can't_
  8. Is the bird under the table? _No, it isn't_
  9. Is the bird behind the door? _No, it isn't_
  10. Is the door shut? _yes, it is_
  11. Is the window open? _yes, it is_
  12. Is the door open? _no, it isn't_
  13. Can Mrs. Cooper see the cat in the room? _yes, she can_
  14. Can Tom see the bird in the yard? _No, He can't_
  15. Can Peter see the bird under the bed? _no, He can't_
  16. Is the bird in Betty's shoe? _yes, it is_
  17. Is the shoe on the chair? _No, it isn't_
  18. Is the bird under the chair? _yes, it isn't_

B. Where's the bed?

floor, bed, on   The bed is on the floor.

Make sentences. Use the words in italics.

■ 1. *bookcase*, in, room   *The bookcase is in the room.*
   2. *bird*, in, yard   ~~the bird in the yard~~
   3. *lamp*, on, table   ~~the lamp on the table~~
   4. in, *boy*, room   ~~the boy is in the room~~
   5. behind, *bird*, curtain   ~~the bird is behind the window~~
   6. Betty, in front of, *Helen*   ~~Betty is in front of Helen~~
   7. desk, in front of, *chair*   ~~the desk is in front of chair~~

─────────── Let's Talk ───────────

Wordgame

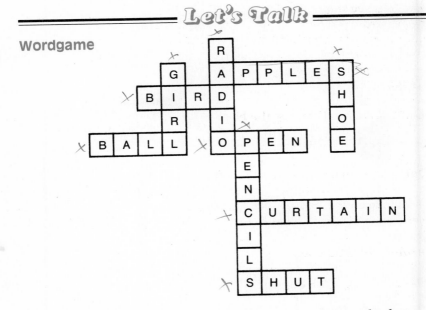

Ask your classmate to guess the answers. Use the words above.

Across →
   She has one apple. He has three.. ~~Apples~~
   The... is in the cage.   ~~the bird is in the cage~~
   He is kicking the... ~~ball~~
   The window is... ~~open~~
   The window isn't.... ~~shut~~ .
   The... is in front of the window.
   ~~curtain~~

Down ↓
   He has a r. ~~adio~~
   She isn't a boy. She's a... ~~girl~~
   The... is black. ~~shoe~~
   He has two pens. She has nine.. ~~pencils~~

Review

Ask and answer questions. Here are some examples.

What can you see in the house? *I can see the Coopers.*

Can you see Betty in the house? *No, I can't.*

Can you see Mr. and Mrs. Cooper? *I can see Mrs. Cooper, but
I can't see Mr. Cooper.*

Vocabulary

Nouns: curtain, poster, room

Adjectives: open, shut

Prepositions: behind, in front of

Conjunctions: and, but

Modals: can, can't

Complete the sentences. Use the vocabulary above.

1. Where's the bookcase? *It's in the* <u>ROOM</u>.
2. Mary is in front of Linda. Linda is <u>behind</u> Mary.
3. The cage is <u>open</u>. Where's the bird?
4. Tom is behind Betty. Betty is <u>in front</u> Tom.
5. The <u>poster</u> is on the wall.
6. I can see a boy, <u>but</u> I can't see a girl.
7. The window is behind the <u>curtain</u>
8. Is the door open? *No, it's* <u>shut</u>.
9. I <u>can't</u> see a man, but I <u>can</u> see a woman.
10. Can you see a lamp <u>and</u> a table?

38 (thirty-eight)

1. **Modals**
   Can you see Peter? Yes, I can.
   Can you see Tom? No, I can't.
   Helen *can* see a lake. She *can't* see a cat.

2. **Conjunctions**
   Tom can see a house, *but* he can't see a yard.
   Helen can't see Tom, *but* she can see Peter.
   Is the lamp on the table *or* under the table?

3. **Prepositions**
   Mrs. Cooper is *behind* Peter. Peter is *in front of* Mrs. Cooper.
   The basket is *under* the table. The TV is *on* the table.
   The TV is *in* the room.

4. **Question word patterns**
   What can you see in Tom's room?
   Where's the mouse?

5. **Adjectives**
   The window is *open*. The door is *shut*.

6. **Simple present**
   Is the window behind the curtain? Yes, it is.
   Is the curtain behind the window? No, it isn't.

4•1 Complete the sentences.

1. Helen, _CAN'T you_ see a poster? *Yes,* _I CAN_
2. _What CAN_ Tom see in the room? *He can see a radio.*
3. Can you see a lamp? _Yes, I CAN_
4. I can see a house, but I _CAN'T_ see a lake.
5. Can Helen see a woman? *Yes,* _she CAN_
6. Can Betty see a guitar? *No,* _she CAN'T_
7. _What_ can Helen see in the picture? _she CAN_ *see a lake.*
8. I can see a man, _but_ I can't _see_ a woman.

4•2 Complete the sentences. Use *in, on, under, behind, in front of.*

1. Where's the boy?
   He's _IN_ the room.
2. Where's the lamp?
   It's _ON the WALL._
3. Where's the cat?
   _It's ON_ the window.
4. Where's the TV?
   It's ON The table.
5. Is the boy on the chair or under the chair?
   He's ON the chair.
6. Where's the girl? _(she's)_
   _____ door.   *the girl is behind the door*
7. Where's the boy?
   _____ TV.
   the boy is in front of the t.v.
   (He's)

4•3 Answer the questions.

1. Is the boy behind the TV? _NO, He isn't_
2. Is the cat behind the window? _NO, It isn't_
3. Is the lamp on the wall? _yes, it is_
4. Is the boy in the room? _yes, He is_
5. Can the boy see the girl? _NO, He CAN't_
6. Is the boy in the chair? _No, He can't ✗ yes, He is_
7. Can the girl see the boy? _yes, she CAN._
8. Can the girl see the TV? _yes, she CAN._

3•1   Complete the sentences.

1. Is this a banana? *No,* __It isn't__.
2. Is that an apple? *Yes,* __it is__.
3. What's __that__ ? *It's an island.*
4. __What's__ that? *It's a motorcycle.*
5. Is the picture on the floor __or__ on the wall?
6. Look __at__ the coat.   It's __in__ the closet.
7. __Look__ at the record player.   __It's__ on the table.
8. __Where's__ the sweater on the bench __or__ on the sofa?
9. __Is__ that a tree? *No,* __it isn't__

3•2   Complete the sentences.

1. This is Roger.   __He is__ Tom's friend.
2. Ann is Elena's friend. __She is__ Betty's friend, too.
3. __What__ color is the shoe? __It's__ *brown.*
4. __What a__ big shoe, Roger!
5. This is Mr. Cooper. __He's__ Tom's father.
6. __What's__ on the floor? __It's__ a record player?
7. This __is__ an airplane. __It's__ big.
8. What's __on__ the wall? __It's__ *a picture.*
   No, __it isn't__. __It's__ *a map.*
9. __is__ this your picture, Tom?
   Yes, __It is__ . __It is__ *my picture.*

3•3   Complete the sentences.

1. __Is__ Luis Tom's brother? *No,* __he isn't__
   __is__ he Tom's friend? __yes,__ *he is.*
2. __How old__ is Betty? __She's__ *eighteen.*
3. Is Betty Colombian? *No,* __she isn't__ __She's__ *American.*
4. This is my English class.   What a __lot of__ students!
5. Elena, __are you__ American? *No,* __I'm__ *Colombian.*
6. __is__ Carol Alan's mother?
   No, __she's__ *Alan's sister.*
7. __is__ this Ted's brother? *Yes,* __she is__
8. __What__ is Ann doing?
   _____ *on the telephone.*
   ANN is talking
   (She's)

Unit Five

5•1

A. Betty is playing beach ball.
What's Peter doing?
He's jogging on the beach.
What's his dog doing?
He's running behind Peter.

Complete the sentences.
- 1. What's Betty doing? *She's playing beach ball.*
  2. <u>What's</u> Helen doing? *She's* <u>playing</u> beach ball, too.
  3. <u>What's</u> Peter <u>doing</u>? *He's* on the beach. He's jogging on the beach
  4. ____ his dog ____? ____ Peter.
  What's   doing   It's running behind Peter

B. Luis is playing volleyball with Tom.
Is Tom playing volleyball on the beach? *Yes, he is.*
Is Peter sitting on the beach? *No, he isn't.*

Complete the sentences and answer the questions.
- 1. Is Helen sitting on the bench? *No, she isn't.*
  2. <u>Is</u> Betty <u>playing</u> with Helen? yes, she is
  3. <u>Is</u> Peter <u>jogging on the</u> beach? Yes, He is
  4. <u>is</u> the dog <u>*</u> in front of Peter? *running No it isn't
  5. <u>is</u> Luis <u>volleyball</u> Tom? yes, He is
            playing   with

C. What's Mr. Cooper doing?
Helen is throwing the beach ball to Betty.
Betty is catching the beach ball.
Mr. Cooper is walking to the ocean.

42 (forty-two)

Present progressive
throwing = LANZANDO
CATCHING = atapando
Walking = caminando

Complete the sentences and answer the questions.

■ 1. What's Betty doing? *She's catching the beach ball.*
  2. *What's* Helen doing? _____ *Betty.* *She is playing ~~~~~ throwing the beach ball to betty*
  3. *What's* Luis *doing*? _____. *He playing volleball with Tom*
  4. _____? _____ *the ocean.* *What's mr cooper doing He's walking to The ocean*

D. What's Peter doing now?
What's Mr. Cooper doing now? *Now he's walking to the beach.*
Is Tom running now? *No, he's holding the volleyball now.*
What's Peter doing now? *He's now jogging.*

Complete the sentences.

■ 1. Betty isn't sitting now. She's playing beach ball now.
  2. *Now* is Peter holding the volleyball? *WHAT*
    No, *NOT* he's jogging.
  3. Helen *is* reading now. She's *NOT* with Betty *NOW*.
  4. What's Tom doing *NOW*? *He's* the volleyball *NOW*.
  5. *How's* catching the beach ball? No, he's *NOW* walking *to the ocean*
    What's

E. What are you doing?
play: I'm *playing* volleyball.

holding = reteniendo

Make sentences. Use any of these words:
ocean, beach ball, volleyball, beach, Tom.

■ 1. catch: *I'm catching the beach ball.*
  2. walk: _____. *I'm WALKING to the OCEAN.*
  3. look: _____. *I'm LOOKING At the beach.*
  4. hold: _____. *I'm holding the*
  5. play: _____. *I'm playing the volleyball NOW*
  6. jog: _____. *I'm jogging on the beach ball.*
  7. throw: _____. *I'm throwning*

hold = sostener
Throw = lanzar

════════════ **Let's Talk** ════════════

What's the code?

Key:	Play with	Jog to	Look at
	Throw	Hold	Catch
	the beach ball	the ocean	the volleyball

Find the code. Here's a hint: ⌐+⌐: *Play with the volleyball.*
  ⌐+⌐:   □+⌐:
  ∟+⊓:   ⊔+⊓:
  ⊏+⌐:   ∟+⌐:

A. She's looking out the window.

Mrs. Cooper is in the house. She's looking out the window. She can see the car in front of the house. She can't see the yard. It's behind the house. She can't see Mr. Cooper, Peter or Betty. Mr. Cooper is standing in the garden. He's looking at the flowers. Peter is in the garden, too. He is looking at the sky.

Answer the questions.

■ 1. What's Mrs. Cooper doing? *She's looking out the window.*
2. Can she see the car? *yes, She can*
3. Where's Mrs. Cooper? *She's in the house* *sky = cielo*
4. Where's the car? *It's in front of the house*
5. Can Mrs. Cooper see the yard? *No, she can't*
6. Where's the yard? *It's behind the house*
7. Where's Mr. Cooper? *He's on the garden*
8. Is he sitting? *yes, He is*
9. Can Mrs. Cooper see Betty? *No, she can't*
10. What's Mr. Cooper looking at? *He's looking at the flowers*
11. Where's Peter? *He's in the garden, too.*
12. Is Peter looking at Mr. Cooper? *No, He is looking at the sky*

44 (forty-four)

escuchar *jugando*

B. I'm playing a record.

MRS. COOPER: Betty, are you playing in the yard?
BETTY: No, mother. I'm in my room. I'm playing a record.

Complete the sentences.
■ 1. MRS. COOPER: Betty, what are you doing?
   BETTY: I'm playing a record.
2. MRS. COOPER: Peter, *Are you* playing volleyball with Tom?
   PETER: No, *Mother.* Tom *is* ₚ ball at the beach. *is playing*
3. MRS. COOPER: John, *looking* the flowers now? *Are you Looking*
   MR. COOPER: Yes, _____ in the garden now. *I'm standing*
4. MR. COOPER: Jane, *can you* see the car in front of the house?
   MRS. COOPER: Yes, *I M . looking* the window now.
   I'm *looking* the car. *I can I can't behind*
      at *I looking at the window now*

C. She isn't looking at the flowers.

Mr. Cooper is in the yard. He's sitting under a tree. Tom is standing
in the garden, but he isn't standing on the flowers. Mrs. Cooper is
looking out the window, but she isn't looking at the flowers. She's
looking at the car. Betty is playing baseball in the yard now. She isn't
playing records in her room. She's throwing the ball to Peter.

Complete and make sentences.
1. Tom isn't playing baseball *with* Peter.
2. Mrs. Cooper is looking *out* the window.
3. Tom isn't standing *on* the flowers.
4. Mr. Cooper isn't standing *under* a tree.
5. Now Peter is throwing the baseball *to* Betty.
■ 6. Tom, standing, flowers   *Tom isn't standing on the flowers.*
7. Luis, throwing the ball, Tom. *Tom is throwing the ball to Luis*
8. Mr. Cooper, standing, tree *Mr Cooper isn't standing under a tree.*
9. Mrs. Cooper, looking, flowers *Mrs cooper isn't Looking the flowers*
10. Betty, playing, baseball *Betty is playing baseball in the yard now.*
11. Mr. Cooper, sitting, tree *Mr cooper sitting under a tree*
12. Mrs. Cooper, looking, car
   At
   MRS cooper is Looking the car

Let's Talk

Your house
Tell a classmate what's in your house.
   A... , an... .

Tell your classmate to draw the house. Fill in the details.
   This is a brown door. This is... .

lyng = en casa   Sick = enfermo

Laughing = Riendo
BARKING = LADRANDO

5·3

espere un minuto

A. Wait a minute!

Betty is sick.   She's lying in bed.
  She is not sleeping.
Helen is looking out the
  window.

BETTY: What are you looking at?
HELEN: I'm looking at your father.
  He's cooking hamburgers in the yard.
BETTY: Is Peter in the yard, too?
HELEN: Yes, he is.   He's playing with Alan.
BETTY: Can you see Elena?
HELEN: No, I can't.   Oh, wait a minute!
  Yes, I can.   She's standing behind the bush.
BETTY: What's she doing?
HELEN: She's laughing at the dog.
BETTY: What's the dog doing?
HELEN: He's barking at Tom.   Tom has the dog's stick.
BETTY: Where's Luis?   Is he playing, too?
HELEN: Oh, no.   Luis is lying under the tree.   He's reading!

Complete the sentences and answer the questions.

■ 1. What's Helen doing?   *She's looking out the window.*
  2. Mr. Cooper can cook.   He's ____ hamburgers now.   cooking
  3. Peter can play.   He's ____ with Alan now.   playing
  4. Alan can throw.   He's throwing the ball now.   playing
  5. The dog can catch a stick.   He's catching a stick now.
  6. Helen is looking at Betty's father.
  7. The dog is barking at Tom.
  8. Luis is lying under the tree.   (Lying)
  9. He is reading!
  10. Elena is standing behind the bush.   standing
  11. What's Betty doing?   She's lying Laughing lying the bed
  12. BETTY: What are you looking at, Helen?
                        I'm looking at your father

46 (forty-six)

B. Betty is sick.
Statement: Mr. Brown's sick.
Question: Is Mr. Brown sick?

Make questions.
- 1. Betty's sick. *Is Betty sick?*
  2. Betty is lying in bed. *Is Betty lying in bed.*
  3. Mr. Cooper is cooking. *Is Mr. C. cooking*
  4. Tom is in the garden. *Is Tom in the garden*
  5. Helen can see Elena. *Can see H*
  6. The dog's barking at Tom. *Is the dog BARKING At tom?*
  7. She's laughing at the dog. *Is she laughing at the dog*
  8. Luis is reading. *Is Luis reading?*

C. Please, be quiet!
ELENA: Tom, please come here. Catch the ball.
TOM: Please, be quiet! I'm reading.
HELEN: And I'm drawing, Elena.
ELENA: What are you drawing?
TOM: Are you drawing your dog?
HELEN: No, I'm not drawing my dog. He's barking at the cat.
ELENA: You're drawing the house!
HELEN: No, I'm not.
TOM: You're drawing Elena.
HELEN: No, I'm not. Look!
ELENA: It's Tom!
TOM: What a good drawing!

drawing = dibujar / locar
BARKing = LADRANDO
Laughing = Riendo
Lying = acostada.
bush = arbusto

Complete the sentences.
- 1. Tom, *Please* come here. *please*
  2. *Be* quiet, *Please.*
  3. Tom's *reading* a book.
  4. Helen *drawing* a picture.
  5. Helen *Isn't* drawing Elena.
  6. Elena, what a good *drawing*!

What are the words?
Complete the words. Answers vary.
bo.o.k	*bARr* king
si.N.g	.st.ick
la.u.g *Laughing*	dra.wing
bu.sh	wa.it. WAIT.
w...w	c.At.ching
window	

Grammar: Items 2, 5, and 6   (forty-seven) **47**

Review

Ask and answer questions.   Here are some examples.
What's this woman doing? *She's lying on the beach.*
What's that man doing? *He's throwing a beach ball to his friends.*
Is he running to the ocean? No, He isn't.

Vocabulary
Nouns: baseball, bush
Verbs: is doing, is drawing, is lying, is sitting, is throwing
Adjectives: sick
Prepositions: at, out, with

Complete the sentences.   Use the vocabulary above.
1. Luis is looking _out_ the window.   At
2. Tom _is throwing_ the beach ball.
3. The woman _is sitting_ on the chair.
4. What _is_ he _doing_? *He is drawing a picture.*
5. Betty's _sick_.   She _is lying_ in bed.
6. Tom's playing baseball _with_ Luis.
7. Peter's in the yard.   He's behind the _bush_.
8. Tom has Peter's _baseball_
9. I'm looking _at_ a picture.

48 (forty-eight)

Grammar

1. **Question word patterns**
   Betty, what are you doing?   What am I doing?   I'm drawing Elena.
   What's Tom doing?   He's playing volleyball.

2. **Present Progressive**
   Is he *cooking* hamburgers?   No, he isn't.
   Is she *looking* at the car?   No, she isn't.

   He *isn't cooking* hamburgers now.
   She *isn't looking* out the window now.

3. **Prepositions**
   Betty's playing ball *with* Helen.
   She's throwing the ball *to* her friend.

   Peter's looking *out* the window.
   Mr. Cooper is looking *at* Peter.

   Alan is running *behind* the house.
   Tom is sitting *in front of* the house.

   Mrs. Cooper is *in* the house.

   Elena is lying *on* the beach.

   Luis is standing *under* the tree.

4. **Adverbs**
   She's running *now*.   Is she running *now*?
   Now she's running.   *Now* is she running?
   She's *now* running.   Is she *now* running?

5. **Modals**
   Can he cook?   Yes, he *can*.
   Can she see the car?   No, she *can't*.

6. **Commands**
   Be quiet, please.
   Please, wait a minute.

5•1   Complete the sentences.

1. Is Peter jogging on the beach? *Yes,* _He is_.
2. Is the dog running in front of Peter? *No,* _It isn't_
3. Is Tom standing behind the house? *No,* _He isn't_
4. Is Betty holding the beach ball? *Yes,* _She is_
5. What are you doing? *I'm playing beach ball* _with_ *my friend.*
6. _What's_ *Tom doing? He's throwing the beach ball* _to_ *Helen.*
7. _What's_ *Mr. Cooper doing? He's walking* _to_ *the ocean.*
8. *I'm playing volleyball* _with_ *Peter.*
9. _What's_ *Peter doing now?* _Now_ *he's catching the beach ball.*

5•2   Complete the sentences.

1. I can't see the beach ball. *It's* _on_ *the ocean.*
2. Mr. Cooper can see the car. *It's* _in front_*of the house.*
3. Mr. Cooper can see Peter. *He's sitting* _on_ *the beach.*
4. Tom is looking _at_ *the flowers.*

Make sentences.

5. Peter, sitting, floor. _Peter is sitting on the floor_
6. Betty, looking, flowers. _Betty is looking at the flowers_
7. Luis, running, bush. _Luis is running behind the bush_
8. Linda, playing, volleyball.
9. Tom, looking, window. _Tom is looking out the window ._

5•3   Read the paragraph.   Answer the questions.

Helen is playing in the yard.   She's throwing a ball to Elena now.
Mrs. Cooper is reading a book.   She's sitting under a big umbrella.   Peter
is looking at a picture.   He's laughing.   Tom is laughing, too.   He's
standing behind Mr. Cooper.

1. What's Mrs. Cooper doing? _Mrs cooper is reading a book_
2. Where's Tom now? _He's standing behind mr cooper_
3. What's Tom doing? _He's laughing._
4. Where's Helen? _She is playing in the yard._
5. What's Helen doing now? _She's throwing is ball to ELENA NOW._
6. Is Elena playing ball? _Yes, she is_
7. Is Mrs. Cooper laughing? _No, she isn't_
8. Where is Mrs. Cooper sitting now? _She is sitting under a big umbrella_

50 (fifty)

4•1 Complete the sentences.

1. _CAN_ Helen see the lamp? *No, she* _CAN'T_.
2. _CAN_ Betty see Helen? *Yes,* _She CAN_
3. _CAN_ Peter see an apple and an orange?
   He _CAN see_ *an apple, but he can't* _see_ *an orange.*
4. _CAN_ you see a boy and girl?
   I can see a girl, but _____ *a boy.*
   I CAN'T see

4•2 Make and answer the questions.

1. bush, bird, see, What, can _WHAT CAN you see a bush an d a bird_
   What can you _see_?
   I can see a _bush_, _but I CAN't see a bied._
2. What, can, see, bowl, apple _What can you see a bowl and an Apple_
   What _____? _CAN you see?_
   I CAN see A bowl, but I CAN't see an Apple
3. What, can, see, room, poster _What CAN you see a room and a pooter_
   _____? _What CAN you see?_
   _____. _I CAN see a Room, but I CAN't see a pooter_
4. What, can, see, basket, book _What CAN you see a basket and a book_
   _____? _WHAT CAN you see?_
   _____. _I CAN see a basket, but I CAN't see a book_

4•3 Complete the sentences.

1. Hey, the cage is _Here_! Where's the bird?
2. The door isn't open. It's _OPEN_.
3. Is the bird in the shoe? *Yes,* _it is_.
4. Is the shoe under the bed? *No,* _it isn't_

Make questions. Answer with the word in italics.

5. basket, *behind* / in front of, the door
   Is the basket behind the door or in _front_? _of The door_
   It's _behind the door_
6. shoe, under / *on*, the bed
   Is the shoe under _!_ or _____? _the bed or on the bed_
   It's _under the bed_
7. curtain, *in front of* / under, window _Is the curtain, in front of the_
   _____? _window or under_
   It's in front of the window. _the window._

Unit Six

A. Plurals

one dog — two dogs one record — two records one chair — two chairs	one book — two books one hat — two hats one map — two maps
Sound of the plural s is / z /	Sound of the plural s is / s /

Give the sound of the last letter. Use / z / or / s /.

■ 1. rooms — / z /
2. radios — _z_
3. letters — _s_
4. birds — _z_
5. cats — _s_

6. volleyballs — _z_
7. sticks — _s_
8. boys — _z_
9. lamps — _s_
10. trees — _z_

B. How many?

Count the cassettes:
one, two, . . .
How many cassettes can you see?
I can see seven.

RECORDING

Answer the questions.

■ 1. How many clocks can you see? *I can see two.*
2. How many guitars can you see? I CAN see three
3. How many drums can you see? I can see four
4. How many pianos can you see? I can see one

Look around your classroom.   Ask and answer *How many* **questions.**

■ 1. desks: *How many desks can you see?*   *I CAN see one*
2. students: _____?   *I CAN see eight*
3. windows: _____?   *I CAN see four*
4. eraser: _____?   *I CAN see one.*

top = Sy per nice
middle = en el medio

C. Tom's room.

HELEN: Where is Tom?
BETTY: He's at the studio.   He's recording a record.
HELEN: I see.   *acerca de, locaule, casi*
BETTY: Tom's crazy about music.
HELEN: Really?
BETTY: Yes.   See the posters on the
walls?   He has six.   And look at his
stereo.   Now look at his bookcase.
Look at the top shelf.   How many
cassettes can you see?
HELEN: Three cassettes and one tape
recorder.
BETTY: Right.   Now look on the middle shelf.
How many cassettes can you see?
HELEN: Eighteen.   You're right.   He is crazy about music.

Answer *Yes* or *No.*

■ 1. Helen is in Tom's room. *Yes*
2. Tom is recording in his room. *NO*
3. Tom is crazy about music. *yes*
4. Tom has two tape recorders. *No*
5. Betty can see the stereo. *yes*
6. Tom has nineteen cassettes in his bookcase. *No*

Ask *How many* questions.

■ 1. How many records can Helen see? *Nineteen*
2. _____? *Twenty-one*   *How MANY records CAN Helen see?*
3. _____? *One*   *How many records can tellen see?*
4. _____? *Six*   *How many records can Helen see.*

Let's Talk

How many?

Read the problems to a classmate.
- Fifteen cassettes.   Five in a box.   How many boxes?
  How many cassettes in four boxes?
- Ten records.   Two records in an album.   How many albums?
  Seven albums.   How many records?
- Three hours per album.   How many hours for seven albums?

A. These aren't tables.

LINDA: These are Tom's albums.
ROLAND: No, these aren't.
These are my albums.

Complete the sentences. Use *this* or *these*.

- 1. This is a table. _This_ isn't a chair. *This*
  2. _These_ are red albums. _these_ aren't blue albums.
  3. _These_ are big pictures. _these_ aren't small pictures.
  4. _This_ isn't a small guitar. _this_ is a big guitar.
  5. _this_ is my tape recorder. _this_ isn't your tape recorder.
  6. _these_ aren't your books. _these_ are my books.
  7. _this_ isn't Tom's radio. _this_ is Roland's radio.
  8. _these_ aren't his records. _these_ are her records.
  9. _these_ are small posters. _these_ aren't big posters.
  10. _this_ isn't an American car. _this_ is an Italian car.

Complete the sentences.

- 1. This _is_ my house. *is*
  2. These _are_ your cassettes.
  3. _this_ is a small radio.
  4. _these_ are white birds.
  5. This _is_ a good book.
  6. These _are_ small umbrellas. These are big umbrellas.
  7. This _is_ a small piano. This is a big piano.
  8. These _are_ big trees. These are small trees.
  9. These _are_ green pencils. These are red pencils.
  10. This _is_ a clean shirt. This is a dirty shirt.
  11. This _is_ your car. _this is_ my car.
  12. These _are_ my pens. _these is_ your pens.
  13. _These are_ blue bicycles. These are green bicycles.
  14. _this is_ a good record. This is a bad record.
  15. _this_ is Roland's guitar. _this is_ Tom's guitar.

54 (fifty-four)

B. Can't you see four people?

Can't you see two buildings?
No, I can't.
Can't you see five chairs?
Yes, I can.

Complete and answer the questions.

■ 1. Can't you see four buildings? *No, I can't.*
2. <u>Can't</u> you see four chairs? <u>NO, I CAN'T</u>
3. <u>Can't you</u> two tables? <u>Yes, I can</u>
4. <u>Can't you</u> four people? <u>NO, I CAN'T</u>

*ce lot of = una grun
CANTidap/*

C. Betty is visiting Elena now.

Betty is looking at Elena's bookcase. She can see a lot of things in the
bookcase.

Complete the dialogue.

■ 1. ELENA: <u>Come</u> here, Betty. <u>Look</u> at my bookcase. *Come; Look*
These are my records. How many records can you count?
BETTY: I can count six.
2. ELENA: <u>Wait</u> a minute. <u>Stand</u> on this chair.
<u>Count</u> the records now. <u>you can now</u>
3. BETTY: Now I can count ten. Wow! These are good records!

Make commands.

■ 1. records, count, the   *Count the records.*
2. look, at, bookcase, the *look at the bookcase*
3. stand, chair, on, a *Stand on a chair*
4. minute, wait, a *Wait a minute*
5. here, come, Betty *Come here, Betty*

Let's Talk

Thank you for the gift.

give = dar ~ given = donado

album, tape recorder, record, card
expensive, nice, pretty, interesting

Give a gift to a friend. Use the vocabulary above.
This is a... . These are... .   *Thank you for the nice... .*
You're welcome.

4

a e=i u=ai
a=e i
i=ai

6·3

A. I'm counting everything. = cada cosa

Tom is working in Mrs. Martino's
music store. Helen is
visiting the store.

HELEN:
Hi, Tom!
What are you doing?
Everything?
Wow! Can I help you?
Come on.
I can't see!
O.K.
Three.
Two.
Right. Oh! I see a
  customer.
A customer.
She isn't?

TOM:
Hi, Helen!
I'm counting things.
Everything.
Well...
Well, okay. Look on the top shelf.
Stand on this chair.
How many big radios can you see?
How many small radios can you see?
Can you see five radios on this shelf?

A what?
She's not a customer.
No, she's my boss.

Complete the sentences.
■ 1. Tom _____ in Mrs. Martino's music store. *is working*
   2. Helen _____ the store. is visiting
   3. Tom _is_ counting things.
   4. HELEN: What are you doing? Can I help you?
      TOM: Yes, you can.
   5. look on the top shelf.
   6. Stand on this chair.
   7. How many big radios _____? can you see
   8. _____ small radios can you see? How many
   9. Helen, _____ see five radios on this shelf? can you
   10. Oh, Tom, I see a customer.
   11. She's not a customer. She's my boss!

56 (fifty-six)

B. What are these?

What's this?
It's a turntable.

What are these?
They're headphones.

What are these?
They're microphones.

Complete and answer the questions.
■ 1. What are these? *They're pianos.*
■ 2. What's this? *It's a studio.*
3. What are these? *they're stereos.*
4. What's this? *It's turntable.*
5. What're? *they're headphones.*
6. What are? *they're microphones.*

C. Are they tapes?
What are these? Are they cassettes?
No, they aren't. They're tapes.

Complete the sentences.
■ 1. What are these? Are they stereos?
   No, they aren't. They're tape recorders.
■ 2. What are these? Are they cassettes? *Yes, they are.*
3. What are these? are they telephones?
   Yes, They are
4. What are these? are they bicycles?
   No, they aren't. motorcycles.
   they're

─────────── *Let's Talk* ───────────

How do you spell this?
Read these words to a classmate. Have the classmate write the words.

see	throw
stand	bark
walk	am
is	are
do	play
catch	sit
laugh	draw
look	hold

How many mistakes?

Grammar: Items 1, 5, 9

Review

What are these things in Helen's room?

This is a record player. This isn't a... .
These are books. These aren't... .
How many...can you see?

Vocabulary

Nouns: boss, customer, everything

Pronouns: these, this

Verbs: is counting, is helping

Modals: can't

Adjectives: bottom, many

Prepositions: about, in, on

Complete the sentences. Use the vocabulary above.

1. Tom is crazy _____ music. *about*
2. Tom is working _IN_ the music store.
3. Helen *is h* Tom. She is counting _everything_.
4. Mrs. Martino isn't a *cust*. She's Tom's *boss*.
5. My bookcase has a top shelf, a middle shelf, and a _bottom_ shelf.
6. How _many_ drums can you count?
7. _Can't_ you see two drums? *Yes, I can.*
8. Stand _on_ the chair.
9. _this_ is a turntable. This isn't a tape recorder.
10. Are _these_ microphones? *No, they're telephones.*

58 (fifty-eight)

Grammar

1. **Question word patterns**
   How many cassettes can you see?   I can see six.
   What are these?   They're stereos.

2. **Nouns**
   dog — dogs   clock — clocks
   piano — pianos   thing — things
   record — records   cassette — cassettes

3. **Prepositions**
   Look *at* the bookcase.   Look *on* the bottom shelf.

4. **Pronouns**
   These are turntables.

5. **Simple present**
   These *are* microphones.   These *aren't* telephones.
   Are these headphones?   Yes, they *are.*

   Are they drums?   No, they *aren't.*   They're guitars.

6. **Modals**
   Can't you see the top shelf?   Yes, I *can.*

7. **Commands**
   (You) Count the buildings.

8. **Adverbs**
   Now look on the bottom shelf.

9. **Present progressive**
   Tom *is working* in the music store.

Test • Unit 6

6•1 Complete the sentences.

1. Count the records. *How many* ____ records can you see?
I can see ____ seven.
2. ____ bicycles can Helen see? *How many*
____ four. *I can see*
3. ____ stereos can Tom see? *How many*
____ two. *I can see*
4. ____ cassettes can you see? *How many*
____ three. *I can see*

Give the sound of the last letter. Use / s / or / z /.

5. tapes *s*
6. pianos *z*
7. guitars *z*
8. drums *s*   *drums*
9. clocks *s*
10. walls *z*

6•2 Complete the sentences.

1. This *is* ____ my car. This isn't your car.
2. These *are* ____ brown books. There aren't blue books.
3. *these* ____ are your cassettes. *there* ____ aren't my cassettes.
4. *this* ____ isn't my drum. *this* ____ is your drum.
5. These are his records. These *aren't* ____ her records.
6. *this* ____ is Roger's book. *these* ____ are Elena's books.
7. *there* ____ drums can you count?
8. Can't you see three people? *Yes, I can*
9. Can't you count four tape recorders? *No, I can't*
10. How many buildings *can* ____ you count?

6•3 Complete the sentences.

1. Tom, what *are* ____ you doing?
2. One, two, three. I'm *count* ____ everything in the bookcase.
3. She is working *in* ____ the store.
4. *are they* ____ these? *They're records. What are*
5. What are these? *they're* ____ drums?
   Yes, *they are* ____
6. *what* ____ are these? Are *they* ____ numbers?
   No, *they aren't* ____ letters. *they are*
7. ____ these? ____ bowls? *What are are they bowls*
   No, ____. ____ baskets. *they aren't . they are baskets*
8. ____ this? ____ a bicycle?
   what is   this is

Maintaining Skills

5•1 Make questions.

1. Helen, catching, beach ball *Is Helen catching the beach ball?*
2. running, Peter, yard, behind, Tom *Is Peter running behind the yard with tom*
3. playing, Betty, volleyball *Is Betty playing volleyball? with*
4. jogging, Mr. Cooper, on beach *Is Mr cooper jogging on beach)*
X 5. Tom, walking, to ocean *is tom WALKING TO OCEAN?*

5•2 Complete the sentences.

1. Mrs. Cooper is _looking_ out the window.
   She's looking _At_ the car.
2. Mr. Cooper is standing _IN_ the garden.
   He's looking _At_ the flowers.
3. Peter is _iN_ the yard.
   He's looking _At_ the sky.
4. Betty is _iN_ the yard, too.
   She's playing volleyball _with_ Peter.

5•3 Complete the sentences.

X 1. _Please_, be quiet. I'm reading.
2. _WAit_ a minute, please. I'm drawing.
3. Helen, throw the ball, _NoW_.
4. Helen _CAN_ cook. She _h looking_ now.
5. Peter _CAN_ read. He _____ now.
   is reading

Extra!   *I CAN see Helen singing*

Read the questions.

Is this a recording studio? Can you see Tom playing his guitar? Is Roland playing his guitar, too? Is Helen singing? Is Linda playing the piano?

Are these headphones? Are they Tom's? Is this a clock? Is it Helen's? Is he counting the music — one, two, three, four?

Tell what's going on.

This is a recording studio. I can see. tom playing his guitar. Roland is playing his guitar, too. Helen is singing. Linda is playing the piano. Yes, they are. Yep, this is, yep, it is

(sixty-one) **61**

Unit Seven

7·1

A. Are these Tom's records?

Are these Tom's books? *Yes, they are.*
Are these Tom's shoes, too? *No, they aren't. They're Peter's.*

MRS. COOPER: Peter, your room is a mess.
PETER: A mess?
MRS. COOPER: A mess.   Clean it.
PETER: But —
MRS. COOPER: Are these your records?
PETER: No, they're Tom's.
MRS. COOPER: Are these your cassettes?
PETER: No, they're Tom's, too.
MRS. COOPER: Are these your books?
PETER: No, they're Tom's.
MRS. COOPER: Is this your room or Tom's?

Complete the sentences.

■ 1. Are these Peter's cassettes? *No, they aren't. They're Tom's.*
   2. _____ these Peter's books?
     No, _____. _____ Tom's, too.
   3. _____ Peter's records?
     No, _____. _____ Tom's.
   4. _____ Peter's shoes?
     Yes, _____.
   5. _____ Tom's room?
     No, _____. _____ Peter's.

B. Where are Peter's shoes?

Where are Tom's things? *They're in Peter's room.*

Complete the sentences.

■ 1. Where are Tom's records? *They're on Peter's table.*
     Where are Tom's cassettes? _____, too.
   2. Where are Tom's books? _____ on the bed.
   3. Where are Peter's shoes? _____ under the table.
   4. Where's Peter's shirt? _____ on the chair.

C. Peter is in Tom's room.   He's putting things on the shelf.

Where are Tom's shoes?
Where is his tape recorder?
Are his guitars on the bottom shelf?
Is his clock on the wall?

Complete the questions. Then find a place for Tom's things.
■ 1. Where are Tom's radios? *They're on the....*
■ 2. Where is Tom's stereo? *It's on the....*
   3. _____ Tom's books?
   4. _____ Tom's guitars?
   5. _____ cassettes?
   6. _____ poster?
   7. _____ shoes?
   8. _____ tape recorder?
   9. _____ records?
  10. _____ clock?
  11. _____ drums?
  12. _____ shirts?
  13. _____ coat?
  14. _____ motorcycle?

Now complete and answer the questions about Tom's things.
  15. Is his stereo on the table?
  16. Are his drums on the middle shelf?
  17. _____ his guitars on the bottom shelf?
  18. _____ poster on the wall?
  19. _____ his cassettes on the table?
  20. _____ his shirts in the closet?
  21. Is his shoes under the bed?

Answer the questions.
■ 1. What's Peter doing? *He's putting things on the shelf.*
     What are you doing now? *I'm...* reading my book now
  2. Where's Peter?
     Where are you? I'm in English class
  3. Where's Tom's coat? th
     Where's your coat?
  4. Where are Tom's things?
     Where are your things?

═══════════ Let's Talk ═══════════

What are they? Where are they?
Draw your room.
Show a classmate something in your picture.
   This is a...   *Where is your...?*
   There are...   *Where are your...?*

Ask questions about your classmate's picture.

A. What is he doing?

Mr. Brown is going into Mrs. Martino's store. He can see four people. Alan is listening to music. He's playing a tape. Tom is fixing a radio. He's touching the wires together. Linda is watching TV and smiling.

Complete the sentences and answer the questions.
■ 1. What's Alan doing?

    play: *He's playing a tape.*

2. _____ Tom doing?

    fix: _____ .

3. _____ Linda doing?

    watch: _____ .

4. _____ Mr. Brown doing?

    go: _____ .

5. Is Linda watching Tom?
   She's _____ .

6. Is Alan playing the piano?
   He's _____ .

7. Is Mr. Brown going into the house?
   _____ *the store.*

8. Is Tom fixing a tape recorder?

   _____ .

9. Is Mr. Brown touching the door?
   Is he smiling?

10. Is Mrs. Martino holding a stereo?

   _____ .

B. What are they doing?

What are Tom and Mr. Brown doing? *They're fixing things.*

Complete the sentences.

■ 1. What are Mrs. Martino and Peter doing? *They're watching TV.*
   2. _____ Tom doing? _____ *fixing a radio.*
   3. _____ Mr. and Mrs. Cooper doing? _____ *smiling at Tom.*
   4. _____ Alan doing? _____ *to music.*
   5. What are Mr. Brown and Tom doing? _____ *fixing a stereo.*
   6. What's Tom doing? _____ *the wires together.*

C. Where are they going?

She's going out of the school.
She's leaving it.

They're going into the school.
They're entering it.

Complete the sentences.

■ 1. Where are Alan and Tom going?
   They're going into the school.
   They're entering it.
   2. _____ Linda going?
   _____ *school.*
   _____ *it.*
   3. Where are Alan and Tom going?
   They're going _____ the school.
   _____ *entering it.*

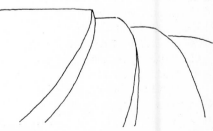

===== Let's Talk =====

What am I doing?

Act out an activity: put on your shoes, comb your hair...
Classmates guess what you are doing.

...is putting on...shoes.
...is combing...hair.

A. His room isn't neat. It's very messy!

Peter's room is a mess. His clothes are all over the room. Everything is very messy.

Tom's room is neat. The floor is neat. The bed is neat. Everything is very neat.

Betty is in her room. Her radio is on her bed. She's listening to music. Her books are all over the desk. Her records aren't on the shelf. They're on the floor. Is her room messy or neat?

Answer the questions.
■ 1. Where are Peter's clothes? *They're all over the room.*
    Is his room very messy or very neat?
  2. Is Tom's bed messy?
    Is his room neat?
  3. Where is Betty?
    What's she doing?
    Where are her books?
    Where are her records?
    Is her room messy or neat?

B. They're playing in Peter's room.

Peter is in his room. He is sitting on the floor. He's fixing his tape recorder. His radio is on. He's listening to music.

But look at Peter's room! It's a mess! His cassettes are lying all over the room. Two cassettes are on the table. Three are under the table. A big record is on the chair. Four small records are on the bed. Two books are on the floor. Peter's friend is jumping onto his bed.

Peter can hear his mother. She's on the stairs. Where can he put his things? He can put the cassettes and records under his bed. He is fixing the mess. Now his mother can't see the mess. Everything is under the bed.

Peter's mother is coming into his room now. She's smiling. The room is very neat.

Complete the sentences.
■ 1. Peter is _____ his room. *in*
  2. He's sitting _____ the floor.
    His friend is jumping _____ his bed.
  3. He's listening _____ the radio.
    The radio is _____.
  4. Is his room messy or _____?
    It's _____.
  5. Things are lying _____ the room.

Complete the sentences.

6. Peter can _____ his mother.
   She's _____ the stairs.
7. Where can he _____ his things?
   He can put _____ under the bed.
8. He's _____ the cassettes under the bed.
   He's _____ the mess.
9. Now he _____ see his mother.
   She's coming _____ the room.
10. Now I _____ see his mother.
    She's going _____ the room.
11. Look at Peter's room now. Is the room_____?
    No, it isn't. It's _____ neat now.

C. Betty is in her room.

PETER: I can see mother. She's going into Betty's room.
BETTY: I can see mother. She's coming into my room.

Complete the sentences.

Betty is going _____ Tom's room. He's sitting
_____ the bed. He's watching her. She's coming _____
his room. Now she's looking _____ his records.
He's crazy _____ music. He's listening _____ his
stereo. He's looking _____ the window. Now
Peter is jumping _____ his bed. Betty is walking
_____ the door. Now she's leaving. She's going
_____ of his room.

═══════════════════ *Let's Talk* ═══════════════════

Where is it going?

Match the number.
> into — _____ .
> out of — _____ .
> onto — _____ .
> under — _____ .
> on — _____ .

Describe where the ball is going. Use the prepositions above.
   Look at the ball. The ball is going from the floor onto the. . . .

Review

Ask and answer questions about the picture.
Where are the books? *They're . . . .* What's Peter doing? *He's . . . .*

Vocabulary
Nouns: mess
Pronouns: they
Verbs: is fixing, is going, is listening
   is putting, are watching

Adverbs: on
Adjectives: neat
Prepositions: all over, in, into

Complete the sentences. Use the vocabulary above.
1. Peter's room is a mess. His cassettes are _____ the floor.
2. Linda _____ to the radio.
3. The radio is _____. They _____ TV, too.
4. Tom _____ the stereo.
5. Helen's room isn't neat. It's a _____!
6. Roland has Tom's guitar. He's going _____ Tom's room.
7. Tom's working _____ the music store.
   He _____ records on the shelf.
8. Are these your books? *No, _____ aren't.*
9. Mr. Cooper _____ out the door.
10. Tom's room isn't messy. It's _____.

68 (sixty-eight)

Grammar

1. **Simple present**
   Are these Tom's books? Yes, they *are*.
   Are these Tom's shoes, too? No, they *aren't*. They're Peter's.

2. **Question word patterns**
   Where are Tom's things? They're in Peter's room.
   What are Alan and Betty doing? They're fixing the radio.
   Where are Peter and Tom going? They're going into the house.

3. **Present progressive**
   Are Linda and Tom *smiling*? No, they aren't. They're *laughing*.

4. **Prepositions**
   They're going *into* the room. They're going *in* the room.
   They're going *out of* the room.

   They're jumping *onto* the bench. They're jumping *on* the bench.

   They're *all over* the room.

5. **Adjectives**
   Is his room *messy*? Is his room *neat*?

6. **Adverbs**
   The radio is *on*.
   Everything is *very* messy.

7•1   Complete the sentences.

1. _____ these Tom's guitars?   *Yes,* _____.
2. _____ stereos?   *Yes,* _____.
3. Where _____ Peter's shoes?   _____ *under the table.*
4. _____ this Alan's tape recorder?   *Yes,* _____.
5. _____ Tom's cassettes?   _____ *on the floor.*
6. _____ Tom's shirt?   _____ *on the chair.*
7. Where _____ Mr. Cooper's car?   _____ *behind the house.*
8. Are _____ Helen's pictures or Betty's pictures?   _____ *Betty's.*

7•2   Complete the sentences.

1. What's Peter _____?   _____ *listening to music.*
2. _____ Peter and Betty doing?   _____ *fixing the radio.*
3. _____ are Tom and Alan going?   _____ *going into the school.*
4. _____ Mrs. Cooper going?   _____ *into the store.*
5. He's going out of the room.   He's _____ it.
6. She's going into the school.   She's _____ it.
7. _____ Tom touching?   _____ *the wires.*

7•3   Read the paragraph.

Linda is in her room.   Her mother is going into the room.   The radio is on.   Linda is listening to music.

Her records are on the shelf.   Her friend is sitting on the floor.   She isn't jumping onto the bed.   Linda's bookcase is very messy.   The books are all over the bookcase.   She is now fixing the books.   Now everything in Linda's room is very neat.

Answer the questions.
1. Where's Linda?
2. Where's her mother?
3. Where are Linda's books?
4. Is her bookcase very neat?
5. What's she doing now?
6. Where's her friend?

6•1 Complete the sentences.

1. _____ the books. One, two, three. How many books _____ see?
2. _____ bicycles can Tom see? _____ *seven.*
3. _____ record players can Helen see? _____ *one.*
4. _____ drums can you see? I _____ *eleven.*

Use / s / or / z / for the sound of the last letter.

5. stores   8. buildings
6. albums   9. cassettes
7. turntables   10. clocks

6•2 Complete the sentences.

1. _____ are Tom's shoes. These _____ John's shoes.
2. _____ is a good record. These _____ bad records.
3. These _____ your books. _____ aren't my books.
4. _____ is a German book. This _____ a French book.
5. These _____ my albums. _____ albums can you count?
6. These _____ apples. I _____ three apples.
7. Can't you see Roger's stereo? *Yes,* _____.
8. This _____ a microphone. These _____ headphones.

6•3 Complete the sentences.

1. Tom is _____ in the store. He's _____ everything: One, two, ...
2. How many drums _____ see? *One, two, three.*
3. _____ these? _____ *bowls.*
4. _____ are these? _____ drums?
   No, _____. _____ *guitars.*
5. _____ are these? _____ headphones?
   Yes, _____.
6. _____ this? _____ a microphone?
   No, _____. _____ *a telephone.*
7. Come on. _____ on the top shelf.
8. My bookcase has a _____ shelf, a _____ shelf, and a _____ shelf.
9. _____ is this? _____ Tom's guitar?
   No, _____. _____ *my guitar.*

Unit Eight

8•1

A. We're the Amoroso family.

We're the Amoroso family.
We're from Mexico. Right
now, we're living in
Chicago. We're having a
good time. We can do many
interesting things here.
We can swim in the lake.
We can visit the Art
Institute. We can see
the tall buildings.

Answer the questions.
■ 1. Are you the Cooper family? *No, we aren't.*
2. Are you from Italy?
3. Are you living in Chicago?
4. Can you swim in the lake?
5. Can you see the tall buildings?

Complete the sentences.
MARIA: Peter and I are at the park.
■ 6. _____ at the park. *We're*
_____ playing football.

CARLOS: José, Tom, and I are in the park, too.
7. _____ in the park.
_____ eating ice cream.

MR. COOPER: Jane and I can sing.
8. _____ can sing.
_____ singing.

MRS. AMOROSO: Pedro and I can play the piano.
9. _____ can play the piano.
_____ playing the piano.

B. We're outside.

John and Jane Cooper are at home. John is working in the yard. Jane is working in the yard, too. Betty is in the house.

BETTY: Peter, are you in the yard?
PETER: No, Carlos and I are in the street. We're looking at Alan's bicycle.
BETTY: Dad? Mom? Where are you?
JOHN: We're outside, Betty. Where are you?
BETTY: I'm inside. I'm with Maria. We're watching TV.
JANE: Watching television! Come outside and help in the yard!

Answer the question.
■ 1. Betty, what are you doing? *I'm watching television.*
2. Carlos, what are you and Peter doing?
3. What is Jane Cooper doing?
4. Where is Maria?
5. Is Peter in the yard?

C. Can you swim? Are you watching television?

PETER:
Can you swim?
Are you watching television?

CARLOS and JOSÉ:
Yes, we can.
No, we aren't.

Answer the questions about Carlos and José.
■ 1. PETER: Carlos and José, are you Colombian?   *No, we aren't.*
2. PETER: Are you Peruvian?
3. PETER: Are you brothers?
4. PETER: Can you read English?
5. PETER: Can you play soccer?

Let's Talk

What can't you do?

Ask two classmates these questions. Can you...
  sleep in a lake?
  work outside?
  cash a check inside your house?
  play baseball in a car?
  drive inside a house?
  swim in a park?
  watch television in a bank?

No, we...
Yes, we...

Grammar: Items 1 and 2

A. It's our house.

JOSÉ: Is this your house, Peter and Betty?
BETTY: Yes, it's our house.
JOSÉ: Is that your car?
PETER: No, our father has our car. He's working.
JOSÉ: Where's your mother?
PETER: Our mother? She's working, too.
JOSÉ: Is this your dog?
PETER: Yes, it's our dog.
JOSÉ: Are these your trees?
PETER: No, they aren't our trees. They're Mrs. Brown's trees.
JOSÉ: Are these your flowers?
BETTY: Yes, they're our flowers.
JOSÉ: Are these your soccer balls?
PETER: No, they aren't. They're Alan's soccer balls.

Complete the sentences.

CARLOS:

■ 1. Is this your street?
2. Is this your house?
3. Are these your flowers?
4. Is this your dog?
5. Are these your trees?

PETER and BETTY:

Yes, it's our street.
Yes, it's our _____.
Yes, _____.
_____.
No, they aren't _____.

B. Are these my footballs?

CARLOS: Are these my footballs?
PETER AND TOM: Yes, they're your footballs.

PETER AND TOM: Are these our footballs?
CARLOS: Yes, they're your footballs.

Make the questions.

■ 1. Are these your records? *Yes, they're our records.*
  2. _____? *No, they aren't our flowers.*
  3. _____? *Yes, she's our sister.*
  4. _____? *Yes, this is our car.*
  5. _____? *Yes, we can see our house.*

C. It's their car.

MARIA: Helen, is this Mr. and Mrs. Cooper's house?
HELEN: Yes, it's their house.
MARIA: Is this their car?
HELEN: No, it isn't their car. It's Mr. and Mrs. Brown's car.
MARIA: Where's the dog?
HELEN: He's sleeping under the tree. He's old.
CARLOS: Are these your new bicycles?
LINDA: Yes, they're our bicycles.
JOSÉ: Can we ride your bicycles?
LINDA: What?
CARLOS: Can we ride your bicycles?
HELEN: O.K. You can take our bicycles.
JOSÉ: Thanks.

Complete the sentences.

■ 1. This is Mr. and Mrs. Cooper's house. It's _____ house. *their*
  2. Carlos and José are riding Helen's and Linda's bicycles. They're riding _____.
  3. Maria is looking at John's and Jane's house. She's looking at _____.
■ 4. Is this your football, Carlos? *No, it's Peter's and Tom's football. It's their football.*
■ 5. Are these your bicycles, Helen and Linda? *Yes, they're our bicycles.*
  6. Are these your radios, John? *No, they're Jane and Betty's radios. They're _____.*
  7. Is this your car, Jane? *Yes, _____.*
  8. Is this your house, Peter and Tom? *Yes, _____.*
  9. Are these your records, Helen and Linda? *No, they're Jane's and Tom's. They're _____.*

Let's Talk

Can you believe it?
Tell a classmate something unusual.
Your classmate is surprised.

  I can run 50 km.   *You're kidding.*
  I can...   *Come on. Really?*

A. You're late, Peter.

JANE: Hello, Peter.

PETER: Hi, Mom!

JANE: You're late, Peter.

PETER: I'm always late because the bus is always late.

JANE: I see.

PETER: Alan is never late. He's never late because he has a bicycle.

JANE: What?

PETER: Alan's never late because he has a bicycle.

JOHN: Open the closet, Peter.

PETER: A bicycle! It's a bicycle! It's a new red bicycle! Wow!

JANE: Take it easy, Peter!

PETER: Wait a minute. Is it Tom's bicycle?

JANE: No, it isn't.

PETER: Is it Betty's?

JANE: No, and it isn't your father's. It's your bicycle, Peter.

PETER: Oh, Mom. Thanks!

JANE: Thank your father, too.

PETER: Thanks, Dad. I can get home on time now.

JOHN: You can get to school on time, too.

PETER: Can I ride my new bicycle outside, now?

JOHN: All right, but be careful.

Complete the sentences.

■ 1. Peter is always late. Alan is _____ late. *never*

2. PETER: I'm always late _____ the bus is always late.
   Alan's never late _____ he has a bicycle.

3. JANE: _____ it easy, Peter. It's your bicycle.
   It's _____ you.

4. JOHN: You can _____ home on time now.
   You can get _____, too. _____ right.
   You can ride your bicycle outside, but _____.

76 (seventy-six)

B. It is sitting in its cage.

bird — its   José and Carlos — their
Helen — her
John — his

Make sentences.
- 1. Helen, counting, records   *Helen is counting her records.*
  2. José and Carlos, reading books
  3. John Cooper, cleaning, car
  4. Bird, leaving, cage

C. What are you doing?

JANE: What are you doing?
  Are you playing?
BETTY and TOM: No, we aren't.
  We're reading our newspaper.
PETER: Yes, I am.
  I'm riding my new bicycle.

Make and answer questions.
- 1. BETTY and TOM: We're reading our newspaper.
    Are you reading your newspaper? Yes, we are.
- 2. PETER: I'm riding my bicycle.
    Are you riding your bicycle? Yes, I am.
  3. BETTY: I can swim.
  4. TOM and PETER: We can play football.
  5. JANE: John and I are looking at our car.
  6. JOHN: I'm reading my newspaper.
  7. PEDRO and ANNA AMOROSO: We're eating our ice cream.

Let's Talk

At the store.

You're in a store. A person is taking your friend's package. Stop
the person. Explain that it is your friend's package.

  Excuse me. This isn't
    your package.   *Yes, it's my package.*
  No, it isn't your package.
    It's my friend's...   *But...*

Your friend:
  It's O.K. That isn't my package. This is my package.

Grammar: Items 1, 2, and 5

Review

Make sentences. Here are some examples.

She's cleaning her car. They're cleaning their car.

Vocabulary

Nouns: newspaper

Adverbs: inside, late, never, outside

Verbs: get

Expressions: at home, be careful on time, right now

Complete the sentences. Use the vocabulary above.

1. Peter has a bicycle. Now he can get _____.
2. Mom, can I ride my new bicycle? *All right, but* _____.
3. Elena is always on time for school. She's never _____.
4. Mr. and Mrs. Cooper are in the yard. They're _____.
5. Betty and Peter are in Tom's room. They're _____.
6. Peter is always late. He's _____ on time.
7. Yoshio is always late. He can't _____ to school on time.
8. Mr. Cooper is reading the _____.
9. The Coopers aren't visiting the Amorosos. They're _____.
10. Come _____. We're late.

Grammar

1. Pronouns

	AMOROSOS	PETER
Are *you* from Mexico?	Yes, *we* are.	No, *I'm* not.
Are *you* visiting New York?	No, *we* aren't.	Yes, *I* am.
Can *you* swim?	Yes, *we* can.	Yes, *I* can.
Can *you* read Chinese?	No, *we* can't.	No, *I* can't.

2. Adverbs

We're *outside*, Betty. Where are you? I'm *inside*.
Peter's *always* late. He's *never* on time. He *never* has his watch.

3. Adjectives

Singular — its, my, your, his, her, its
Plural — our, your, their

The bird is singing in *its* cage.
I'm reading *my* newspaper.
You're eating *your* icecream.
He's walking to *his* house.
She's riding *her* bicycle.

We're taking *our* car.
You're watching *your* TV.
They're washing *their* car.

4. Conjunctions

I'm late *because* the bus is always late.

8•1 Complete the dialogue.

MARIA: Are you sisters?
HELEN and BETTY: No, _____.
MARIA: Are you friends, Helen and Betty?
HELEN and BETTY: Yes, _____.
MARIA: Are you Canadian?
HELEN: I _____, but Betty _____.
MARIA: Betty, are you American?
BETTY: Yes, _____.
MARIA: My brother's crazy about music. I can hear his
    stereo. Can _____ hear _____ stereo?
HELEN and BETTY: No, _____.

8•2 Complete the sentences. Use *my, your, his, her, its, our, their.*

1. Elena is Betty's friend. She's Helen's friend. She's _____ friend.
2. This Mr. and Mrs. Cooper's yard. It's _____ yard.
3. Roland, is this your school? *No, it isn't* _____ *school.*
4. Maria and José, is this your father? *Yes, he's* _____ *father.*
5. These are Helen's and Linda's records. They're _____ records.
6. Peter has a baseball. It's _____ baseball.
7. Is this my new record? *Yes, it's* _____ *new record.*
8. Helen is Betty's friend. She's _____ friend.
9. Betty and Peter, is he your brother? *Yes, he's* _____ *brother.*
10. This is my bicycle. This is your bicycle. These are _____ bicycles.

8•3 Read the dialogue.

MRS. MARTINO: Tom, you're late.
TOM: Sorry, Mrs. Martino. I'm late because the bus is
    always late.
MRS. MARTINO: I see. But Roland is never late. He's always on time.
TOM: He's on time because he has a car.
MRS. MARTINO: Oh, all right. Well, these are our new records. Put
    the records and these cassettes on the shelf.
TOM: O.K., Mrs. Martino.

Answer *Yes* or *No.*

1. Tom is at the music store.
2. Mrs. Martino is late.
3. Tom is never late.
4. Tom is always on time.
5. Roland has a car.
6. The bus is always late.

7•1   Complete the sentences.

1. Are _____ radios? *No, _____, _____ stereos.*
2. _____ this your book? *Yes, _____.*
3. Where _____ Peter's cassettes? _____ *under the table.*
4. Are _____ Alan's records? *No, _____.*
5. Where _____ the bicycle? *It's in the yard.*
6. What are _____? _____ *Tom's pictures.*
7. Are _____ your records or my records? _____ *your records.*
8. Is _____ John's sweater? *Yes, _____.*

7•2   Complete the sentences.

1. What _____ Betty touching? _____ *touching an umbrella.*
2. What _____ Tom and Alan touching? _____ *touching the TV.*
3. Roland is going into Tom's room. He's _____ the room.
4. Linda and Alan are going out of the room. They're _____ the room.
5. Where is Peter going? *He's _____ into Tom's room.*
6. Where are Linda and Peter going? *They're _____ out of the room.*
7. _____ Linda holding her book? *Yes, _____.*
8. _____ Elena smiling at Peter? *No, _____.*

7•3   Complete the sentences.

1. Alan's things are all _____ his room.
2. Is Alan's room neat? *No, it isn't. It's _____.*
3. Elena is _____ to music. Her radio is _____.
4. What's Roger _____? *He's _____ TV.*
5. The dog is jumping _____ the bed.
6. Where are Betty's records? _____ *bottom shelf.*
7. Are _____ Tom's cassettes? *No, _____.*
8. Peter's room is _____ messy. It's not _____ neat.
9. Where _____ Peter's shoes? _____ *under the bed.*

Unit Nine

A. They're buying a record.

Mr. and Mrs. Cooper are in Mrs. Martino's music store. They're buying a new guitar. It's a birthday present. It's for their son, Tom. He's crazy about music.

Maria and Carlos are in the store, too. They're buying a record. It's for Helen. She's crazy about music, too.

Complete the sentences.
■ 1. Where are Mr. and Mrs. Cooper? *They're in the music store.*
2. What are Mr. and Mrs. Cooper doing? _____ *a guitar.*
3. Where are Maria and Carlos? _____ *in the store, too.*
4. What are Maria and Carlos _____? _____ *record.*
5. The Coopers _____ a new guitar.
6. It's _____ their son, Tom.
  It's a _____ present.
7. Maria and Carlos _____ in the store, too.
  _____ a record. _____ Helen.
  They're buying a record because Helen's _____ music.

B. Who's this?

Who is this? *It's Peter. He's riding his bicycle.*
Who's this? *It's Mr. and Mrs. Cooper. They're reading their newspaper.*

Who's this? Complete the sentences. Use the names.
■ 1. Alan and Roland:
  It's Alan and Roland. They're drawing.
2. Maria:
  It's _____. _____ *swimming.*
3. Tom:
  _____. _____ *eating ice cream.*
4. Elena and Linda:
  _____. _____ *swimming.*
5. Mr. and Mrs. Amoroso:
  _____. _____ *buying presents.*
6. Mr. and Mrs. Cooper:
  _____. _____ *jogging.*

C. Let's go home now.

Jane and John Cooper are in a bookstore. They're buying books.
JANE: Look, John. Let's buy the newspaper, too.
JOHN: That's a good idea.
JANE: Let's go home now.

JOHN: No, let's not. The weather is bad. Let's wait.
JANE: Oh, it's raining. We can read the newspaper here.
JOHN: Look. The weather is clearing up now. It isn't raining.
JANE: O.K. Now we can go home.
JOHN: Yes, let's.

Complete the sentences and answer the questions.

- 1. Let's buy the _____, too. *newspaper*
  2. That's a _____.
  3. We _____ home now. _____ go.
  4. No, _____ not. The _____ is bad.
  5. Oh, it's _____.
  6. It isn't raining now. The weather _____.
  7. Now we _____ home.
  8. Yes, _____.
- 9. Where are the Coopers? *They're in a bookstore.*
  What are they doing?
  10. Is the weather good?
  Is it clearing up now?

Make requests with *let's* or *let's not*. Answers 1–6 vary.

- 1. watch: *Let's watch TV.*
- 2. buy: *Let's not buy presents.*
  3. play: _____.
  4. go: _____.
  5. ride: _____.
  6. visit: _____.

Complete the sentences.
The Coopers are at home. They're talking about the evening.

- 1. JANE: _____ watch TV. *Let's*
  2. JOHN: No, _____. Let's visit my mother.
  3. JANE: No, _____. _____ visit my mother.
  4. JOHN: No, _____ visit your mother or my mother.
  _____ watch TV.

═══════════════ Let's Talk ═══════════════

What can we do tonight?
Exchange suggestions with a classmate.

Let's go to a restaurant. *No, let's not. Let's watch TV.*
No, let's not. Let's... . *No, let's not. Let's... .*

Finally:
Let's... .
O.K.

A. They're practicing.

This is Tom's band. His friends are practicing in his garage now.
What instruments are they playing? Tom is playing guitar. Roland is
playing guitar, too. Betty is playing drums. Linda is playing organ.
And who is singing? Helen is. Mr. and Mrs. Cooper are listening to the
band.

Complete the sentences.
■ 1. What's Betty playing? *She's playing drums.*
2. What are Tom and Roland playing? *They're _____.*
3. _____ Linda playing? *She's playing organ.*
4. _____ Helen doing? *She's singing.*
5. _____ Tom's friends doing? *They're practicing.*

B. Who's singing?
Who's playing guitar? *Tom and Roland are.*

Answer the questions.
■ 1. Who's practicing? *Tom's band is.*
■ 2. Who's practicing? *Tom's friends are.*
3. Who's listening to the band?
4. Who's singing?
5. Who's playing guitar?
6. Who's playing drums?
7. Who's playing organ?

C. What are they doing in the first picture?

Maria and Helen are looking at pictures of Betty and Maria in a photograph album. They're doing many things in the photographs. In the first picture, they're playing soccer with Alan. In the second picture, they're sitting in the park. In the third picture, they're watching TV. They're singing with Tom's band in the fourth picture. They're standing in front of the bookstore in the fifth. In the last picture, they're swimming in the lake.

Complete the sentences.
■ 1. MARIA: Helen, look at these pictures. Betty and I are doing many things. In the first picture, _____ playing soccer with Alan. *we're*
  2. In the third picture, we're _____.
  3. In the fourth picture, _____.
  4. _____ in the park in the second picture.
  5. _____ in front of the bookstore.
■ 6. MARIA: Tom, look at these pictures.
     Look. You're playing soccer with Alan _____ picture. *in the first*
  7. You're _____ TV in the third picture.
  8. Now, _____ with Tom's band.
     You're singing _____.
  9. Now, _____ in the park.
  10. _____ the bookstore.
  11. _____ the lake.

Make sentences. Use *he, she, we, you* and *they*.
■ 1. John and I, eat, ice cream   *We're eating ice cream.*
  2. Helen and you, read, books
  3. John and Dan, play, soccer
  4. Don, kick, ball
  5. Helen, buy, presents

━━━━━━━━━━ Let's Talk ━━━━━━━━━━

Who's where?
You're the teacher. Make a seating chart. Put desks in rows. Put names on the desks.

Who's in the first row?	...are
Who's in the second row?	...are
Who's in the third desk in the first row?	...is
Who's in the...?	
Finally, who's in the last...?	

Grammar: Items 1 and 5

A. Who are Alan and Roger?

Tom's band is inside. The musicians are practicing in his garage. Tom and Roland are playing guitar. Betty is playing drums. Linda is playing organ and Helen is singing.

Alan and Roger are outside. They're Tom's friends but they aren't in the band. They're sitting on the porch. They aren't enjoying the music because they can't hear the instruments. They can't play soccer because it's raining. They can't go home because it isn't clearing up. They're bored.

Complete the sentences.
■ 1. Who is this? *It's Alan.*
   2. _____ is Alan? *He's Tom's friend.*
   3. _____ is this? _____ *Alan and Roger.*
   4. _____ are Alan and Roger? _____ *Tom's friends.*

B. Who? Where? What?

Who are they? Where are they? What are they doing?

Complete the sentences.
■ 1. Where is Tom's band? *It's inside.*
   2. _____ the musicians doing? _____ *practicing.*
   3. _____ playing guitar? *Roland and Tom* _____.
   4. _____ singing? *Helen* _____.
   5. _____ playing organ? *Linda* _____.
   6. _____ Alan and Roger? _____ *outside.*
   7. _____ they doing? _____ *on the porch.*
   8. _____ bored? *Alan and Roger* _____.
   9. _____ Alan and Roger enjoying the music? *No,* _____.
  10. _____ they play soccer? *No,* _____.

C. He can't. They can't.

Singular	Plural
is — isn't	are — aren't
can — can't	can — can't

Complete and answer the questions.
■ 1. Is Tom's band outside?
   2. _____ the musicians on the porch?
   3. _____ Alan and Roger bored?
   4. _____ it raining?
   5. _____ Helen singing?
   6. _____ Alan and Roger hear the music?
   7. _____ Tom play guitar?

D. Here is the money.

The weather is bad today. It's raining. Mr. and Mrs. Cooper are at home. Mrs. Cooper is reading and Mr. Cooper is watching TV. Peter and Alan are in Peter's room. They can't go outside. They're bored.

PETER: The weather is terrible. We can't ride our bikes, but we can practice our instruments.
ALAN: Oh, let's not.
PETER: Wait a minute. I can hear thunder.
MRS. COOPER: What's making the terrible noise? Are you practicing?
PETER: No, mother. I'm not practicing. The terrible noise is thunder. We're scared.
MRS. COOPER: Oh, I'm sorry. Yes, I can hear the thunder now, too.
ALAN: Well, Peter, what can we do now?
PETER: Look out the window, Alan. It's clearing up.
ALAN: Oh, good. Let's go to the store for ice cream.
PETER: O.K. Here's the money for ice cream.

Make questions. Use *you, he, she, it, they*.
- 1. Peter and Alan, bored   *Are they bored?*
  2. Mrs. Cooper, reading
  3. Mr. Cooper, watching TV
  4. Peter and Alan, practice
  5. Mrs. Cooper, hear the thunder
  6. The weather, clearing up
  7. Peter and I, going to the store
  8. Alan and you, scared
  9. Peter and you, practicing now
  10. Peter and Alan, buying ice cream

Complete the sentences.
- 1. MRS. COOPER: What is making the _____ noise? *terrible*
  2. MR. COOPER: I'm _____ TV.
  3. PETER: Alan, _____ the money for ice cream.
  4. ALAN: Peter, _____ not practice our instruments today.
  5. MRS. COOPER: Oh, I'm _____. I can hear the thunder now.

Let's Talk

What's the occupation?
Think of an occupation.
Ask a classmate a question.
The classmate can guess the job.

Who's always talking on the telephone?   *Telephone operators are.*
Who's always... ?   *Teachers... .*
Who's... ?   *Musicians... .*

Review

Ask and answer questions.

Who's running? *Tom is.* Who's cooking? *The Coopers are.*
Where are Betty and Peter? *They're under the tree.*
Who can hear thunder? *They can.*

Vocabulary

Nouns: band, garage, instrument, piano, porch, weather
Verbs: are buying, is clearing up, is practicing, is raining
Adjectives: scared, terrible

Complete the sentences. Use the vocabulary above.

1. It isn't raining now. It _____.
2. What _____ is Tom playing? *He's playing the guitar.*
3. What a _____ noise! I can't hear the TV.
4. The _____ is bad today. It's raining.
5. Tom and his friends have a _____. They're practicing now.
6. It _____. We can't play outside.
7. Tom's band _____ in his room.
8. The band isn't practicing in the _____.
9. Mr. and Mrs. Cooper _____ a guitar for Tom.
10. What's Linda doing? *She's playing the _____.*
11. I can hear the thunder. I'm _____.
12. Alan and Roger are sitting on Tom's _____.

Grammar

1. **Question word patterns**
   Who's this?　It's Peter.
   　　　　　　It's Mr. and Mrs. Cooper.

   Who's singing?　Maria is.
   　　　　　　　Maria and Helen are.

   Who's Peter?　He's Tom's brother.

   Who are Alan and Roger?　They're Tom's frineds.
   Where are Maria and Carlos?　They're in the store.
   What are they doing?　They're buying a record.

2. **Commands**
   Let's go home now.　Yes, *let's.*
   Let's watch TV.　No, *let's not.*

3. **Prepositions**
   The birthday present is *for* Tom.
   Let's go to the store *for* ice cream.

4. **Present progressive.**
   Is it *clearing up* now?

5. **Pronouns**
   Carlos and I: *We*'re singing
   Carlos and You: *You*'re singing
   Carlos and Helen: *They*'re singing

6. **Adverbs**
   Here is *(Here's)* the money.

9•1   Complete the sentences.

1. Who's this? _____ *Maria. She's reading.*
2. _____ this? _____ *Peter and Alan.* _____ *going home.*
3. _____ this? _____ *Tom.* _____ *drawing.*
4. _____? _____ *the Coopers.* _____ *writing.*
5. _____? _____ *Mr. and Mrs. Amoroso.* _____ swimming.

9•2   Complete the sentences.

1. Who _____ singing? *Peter and Alan* _____.
2. _____ playing guitar? *Betty* _____.
3. _____ Linda and Maria playing? _____ *playing piano.*
4. _____ Betty playing? _____ *drums.*
5. _____ listening? *Mr. and Mrs. Cooper* _____.

Make sentences.   Use *he, we, you, they.*
6. You and Tom, playing drums
7. Betty and Maria, eating ice cream
8. Alan, watching TV
9. The Coopers, buying presents
10. Peter and I, riding bicycles

9•3   Read the dialogue.   Give short answers for the questions.

ROLAND: Who's making noise?
ALAN and PETER: We are.   We're practicing.
ROLAND: What instrument are you playing?
PETER: I'm playing drums and Alan is playing piano.
ROLAND: Oh, I see.   But I can't hear the radio.
ALAN and PETER: We're sorry, Roland.
ROLAND: Tom and I are listening to the radio and we can't hear
   the music.
PETER: O.K., Roland.

1. Who is making noise?
2. Who is playing drums?
3. Can Roland hear the radio?
4. Are Alan and Peter sorry?
5. Who is practicing?
6. Who is listening to the radio?
7. Can Tom and Roland hear the music?

8•1 Complete the sentences.

1. Are you the Amoroso family? *Yes, _____.*
   Are you from Italy? *No, _____.*
   Are you living in Chicago right now? *Yes, _____.*
   Can you swim in the lake? *Yes, _____.*
   Can you run inside? *No, _____.*

8•2 Complete the sentences with *my, your, his, her, our, their.*

1. Is this my new house? *Yes, it is _____ new house.*
2. Peter is Alan's friend. He's Pedro's friend. He's _____ friend.
3. Are these your flowers, Elena? *No, they aren't _____ flowers.*
4. Elena is Betty's friend. She's _____ friend.
5. Peter and Tom, is this your mother? *Yes, she's _____ mother.*
6. Roland has a new baseball. It's _____ baseball.
7. These are Elena's and Roger's footballs. They're _____ footballs.
8. This is Mr. and Mrs. Amoroso's yard. It's _____ yard.
9. Helen and Linda, are these our records? *Yes, they're _____ records.*
10. Is this your house, Carlos? *Yes, it's _____ house.*

Extra!

Read this story about Mrs. A. helping Mr. Z.

This is Mr. Z. He's a musician. He's never late. He's always on time. He's in his studio now because the clock is counting ten.

But he has a mess in his studio. He can't practice because everything is all over the room. First, he can't see his instrument. Where is it? Is it behind the bookcase? Second, where is his music book? Is it under the table? Third, what is he going to do? Last, who can help?

Here is Mrs. A. She's crazy about music. She's coming into the studio. She can fix the mess. First, she's looking behind the bookcase and under the table. Second, she's putting things in order. Third, she's smiling. Last, they're leaving together.

Now change the story. Have Mrs. A and Mrs. B. helping Mr. Y. and Mr. Z.
This is Mr. Y. and Mr. Z. They're . . .

Unit Ten

10·1

A. This is a shopping bag.

This is a chicken.
This is an egg.
This is a big cooky.
This is an orange carrot.
This is a brown egg.
This is a shopping bag.

Complete the sentences.

■ 1. This is _____ carrot. *a*
2. This is _____ big egg.
3. This is _____ old hat.
4. This is _____ small chicken.
5. This is _____ dirty shopping bag.

6. This is _____ orange ball.
7. This is _____ red apple.
8. This is _____ apple.
9. This is _____ egg.
10. This is _____ interesting book.

B. Do you have my new magazine?

Roger and Mary are in the kitchen. Roger has a magazine. He is reading, but he is hungry, too.

ROGER:
Do you have a banana?
Do you have some cookies?
Good. Do you have my new magazine?
Do I have your books?
Here are your books.

MARY:
No, I don't.
Yes, I do.
No, I don't.
Yes, you do.
Thanks.

Answer the questions.

■ 1. Roger, do you have my books? *Yes, I do.*
2. Mary, do you have my new magazine?
3. Mary, do you have some cookies?
4. Mary, do you have a banana?
5. Roger, are you hungry?

C. What else do you have in your bag?

PETER: Hi, Mom! I'm hungry. What do you have in the shopping bag?
MRS. COOPER: I have some cookies and some carrots.
PETER: Betty, what do you have?
BETTY: I have an apple, some bananas, and a chicken.
PETER: What do you have in the box, Betty?
BETTY: I have some cookies.
PETER: What else do you have, Betty?
BETTY: I have some apples.
PETER: What else do you have, Mom?
MRS. COOPER: I have some eggs and some vegetables.

Complete the sentences.

■ 1. What do you have in the bag mother? *I have some carrots.*
   What _____ on the table?
   I _____ *some vegetables.*
  2. _____ in the box Betty?
   _____ *some cookies.*
   What else _____ have?
   I _____ *some apples.*
  3. What _____ I have on the table, Peter?
   _____ *some bananas.*

D. I have a pencil, but I don't have an eraser.

MARY: I have a pencil, but I don't have an eraser.
   Do you have an eraser, Roger?
ROGER: Yes, I do. Hey, I'm hungry. Let's change the subject.
   Do we have ice cream in the kitchen?
MARY: We have apples, but we don't have ice cream.

Complete the sentences.

■ 1. Do you have a motorcycle, Ann and Alan? *We have a bicycle, but we
   don't have a motorcycle.*
  2. Do you have a bag, Betty?
   _____ *basket, but* _____ *bag.*
  3. Do you have a piano, Tom and Betty?
   _____ *guitar, but* _____ *piano.*

Let's Talk

What do you have?

Make a shopping list.
   What do you have on your list?   *I have a . . . .*
   Do you have a . . .   *No, ...*
   Do you have some . . . ?   *Yes, ...*
   What else do you have?

SHOPPING LIST

Grammar: Items 1–4

A. Do they have your records?

HELEN: Do your sisters have some new magazines?
LINDA: Yes, they do.
HELEN: How many do they have?
LINDA: They have three or four.
HELEN: Let's listen to some
  records and read some magazines.
LINDA: We can't. Tom and Peter have
  my records. I'm angry because they
  have my records. They have my
  stereo, too.
HELEN: What else do they have?
  Do they have your radio?
LINDA: No, they don't.
HELEN: Well, let's listen to the radio.

Answer the questions.

■ 1. Do Linda's sisters have some magazines? *Yes, they do.*
   2. Do they have ten magazines?
   3. Do Tom and Peter have Linda's radio?
   4. Do they have Linda's records?
   5. What else do they have?

B. Peter, sit on the chair, please.

Don't sit on the table.
Sit on the chair.

Alan, don't write in your notebook.
Write on the board, please.

Complete the dialogue.

■ 1. ALAN: Let's draw a picture, Peter.
   MR. BROWN: No, don't draw a picture. Write in your notebook.
   2. PETER: Let's sit on the bed, Alan.
   MRS. COOPER: No, _____ sit on the bed. _____ on the chairs.
   3. TOM: Let's listen to the radio, Helen.
   BETTY: No, _____ the radio.
      _____ my records.
   4. HELEN: Let's watch TV, Linda.
   MRS. COOPER: No, _____. _____ some magazines.
   5. ROGER: Let's _____ soccer, Tom.
   TOM: No, _____ soccer. _____ your guitars.

C. Where are they going?

TOM: Where are you going?
JOSÉ: I'm going to the store on the corner.
TOM: Where's Elena going?
JOSÉ: She's going to school.
TOM: Where are Betty and Bill going?
JOSÉ: They're going to the bus stop
   at the corner.

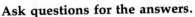

Ask questions for the answers.
■ 1. I'm going to the bookstore. *Where are you going?*
■ 2. Elena's going to school. *Where's Elena going?*
  3. Betty and Mary are going to the shoe store.
     Where _____?
  4. Linda is going to the music studio.
     _____?
  5. Tom and Roger are going into the music studio.
     _____?
  6. Betty is going to the bus stop.
     _____?

D. Linda's school.

   Where's José? Where is he going? José isn't at home. He's at school. The school is on the corner. He's going into his classroom. Some students are standing in the hall. Mr. Brown is sitting at his desk. He is looking out the window. It's raining. His umbrella is in the corner. The teacher can see the bus outside. The bus stop is at the corner. A girl is running into school. She's late because the bus is late.

Answer the questions.
■ 1. Where's José? *He's at school.*
  2. Where is he going?
  3. Where are the students standing?
  4. Where is Mr. Brown sitting?
  5. Where's his umbrella?
  6. Where's the school?
  7. Where's the bus stop?
  8. Where's the girl going?

Let's Talk

Find It!

Give your teacher something with your name on it. Ask your teacher to give you a classmate's possession. Find your possession.
   Do you have my ... ?   *No, I don't. Yes, here it is.*

A. Have you got a pen?

Peter and Tom are going to school. Peter's room is a mess. He's looking for things. Betty and Tom are helping.

PETER: Have you got a notebook?
TOM: Yes, I have. Have you got a pen, Peter?
PETER: No, I haven't. Ask Betty for her pen.
BETTY: I haven't got a pen. Have you got your books?
TOM: Yes, we have. But we haven't got everything.

Complete the sentences.
■ 1. Tom, have you got a pen? *Yes, I have.*
   2. Betty, _____ got a watch?
     Yes, _____.
     _____ your pen?
     No, _____.
   3. Peter, _____ I got your notebook?
     Yes, _____.
   4. Peter and Tom, _____ got your pens?
     No, we _____.
     _____ got your erasers?
     Yes, _____.
   5. _____ Peter and Tom got their notebooks?
     No, _____.
     _____ they got their books?
     Yes, they _____.

B. What have you got in your bag?

BETTY: I've got an apple, but I haven't got an orange.
   What have you got in your bag, Peter?
PETER: I've got a book, but I haven't got a magazine.
   What have you got in your bag, Tom?
TOM: I've got a cookie, but I haven't got a banana.

Complete the sentences.
■ 1. Stereo, radio: What have you got in your room?
     I've got a stereo, but I haven't got a radio.
   2. bike, car: What _____ you got in your garage?
     I've _____ a bike, but I _____ a car.
   3. brother, sister: _____ you got at home?
     _____ a brother, but I _____ a sister.
   4. book, notebook: Tom, _____ got at school?
     _____ a book, but _____ a notebook.

5. bush, tree: Mr. Cooper, _____ got in your yard?
_____ *bush but* _____ *tree.*

C. What a pretty house!

LINDA: Betty, we've got a present for the Browns. Can you give my friend Alan their address? Can you show Alan their house?

BETTY: Yes, of course. It's the house on the corner.

LINDA: What a pretty house! How many rooms have they got?

BETTY: They've got seven rooms. The big room in the front is the living room. The small room behind the living room is the kitchen. They've got a big yard, but they haven't got a garage.

LINDA: You've got a big yard, too. We've got a garage, but we haven't got a big yard.

The Browns
25 Lakeshore Drive
Chicago, IL 60605

Complete the sentences.

■ 1. They've got a kitchen, but they haven't got a garage.
2. _____ got a car, but they haven't got a motorcycle.
3. _____ got a house, but we _____ got a yard.
4. _____ got a big living room, but you _____ got a big kitchen.
5. _____ got their present, but I _____ got their address.

D. Review

Spell these words.

1. a _ p _ e
2. b _ n _ n _
3. c _ r _ o _
4. c _ i _ k _ n
5. s _ m _
6. c _ o _ i _
7. e _ g
8. h _ l _
9. k _ t _ h _ n
10. m _ g _ z _ n _
11. o _ a _ g _
12. s _ h _ o _
13. h _ n _ r _
14. a _ g _ y
15. c _ r _ e _
16. h _ m _
17. e _ s _
18. v _ g _ t _ b _ e _

=========== *Let's Talk* ===========

Take a trip.

Your class is going on a trip with one suitcase.
What have you got in your suitcase?
First Student: Name item. Second student:
Name an item and repeat the first item.
Third student:... , and so on.   *We've got... .*

Review

Ask Betty, Mrs. Cooper and Peter some questions they can answer.
Betty, what do you have in your shopping bag?
What else do you have?
Do you have a banana?

Vocabulary

Nouns: corner, eggs, hall,
living room
Adverbs: please, where

Adjectives: angry, else, hungry,
some

Complete the sentences.   Use the vocabulary above.
1. You have _____ cookies.
2. What _____ do you have?
3. Peter is eating three hamburgers.   He is very _____.
4. _____, don't sit on the table.
5. The shoe store is on the _____.
6. Now Betty has Peter's magazine.   He is _____.
7. The teacher is standing in the _____ at school.
8. Wait a minute.   My books are in the _____.
9. Do they have some _____?
10. _____ is Tom going?

Grammar

1. **Adjectives**
   I have *some* bananas.   I have *a* banana.
   They have *some* apples.   I have *an* apple.

2. **Simple present**
   Do I *have* her pen?   Yes, you *do*.
   Have I *got* her pen?   Yes, you *have*.

   Do you *have* her pencil?   No, I *don't*.
   Have you *got*... ?

   Do we *have* their sweater?   Yes, you *do*.
   Have we *got*... ?

   Do they *have* their coats?   No, they *don't*.
   Have they *got*... ?

   We *have* a yard, but we *don't have* a garage.
   We've *got* a yard, but we *haven't got* a garage.

3. **Question word patterns**
   What do you have in your basket?   I have some carrots.
   What have you got... ?   I've got some.... .

4. **Commands**
   Show her the vegetables. Please, don't show her the cookies.
   Give her the eggs. Don't give her the chickens, please.

5. **Prepositions**
   The school is *on* the corner.
   The bus stop is *at* the corner.
   The umbrella is *in* the corner.

   Linda is *at* school. She isn't *at* home.

10•1   Complete the sentences.   Use *a, an, some.*

1. I have _____ white egg.
2. Alan has _____ orange bike.
3. You have _____ vegetables.
4. I'm reading _____ English book.
5. I'm eating _____ cookie.

6. You have _____ carrots.
7. Betty has _____ old record.
8. You have _____ new stereo.
9. I have _____ apples.
10. I can see _____ magazines.

Complete the sentences.
1. What _____ you have in the shopping bag? *I* _____ *some eggs.*
2. _____ you have some bananas? *No,* _____.
3. _____ you have my books? *Yes,* _____.
4. _____ you have an umbrella? *No,* _____.
5. _____ you have a magazine? *Yes,* _____.

10•2   Complete the sentences.

1. _____ Peter and Alan have bikes? *Yes,* _____.
2. _____ they have some eggs? *No,* _____.
3. _____ Tom and Peter have a dog? *Yes,* _____.
4. _____ they have an old car? *No,* _____.
5. No, _____ watch TV.   Listen _____ the radio.
6. No, _____ go to the store.   _____ to school.
7. Where _____ you going? *I'm* _____ *home.*
8. Where _____ Peter going? *He's going* _____ *school.*
9. _____ the bus stop? *It's* _____ *the corner.*
10. Where _____ Peter and Alan going? *They* _____ *going to the shoe store.*

10•3   Complete the sentences.

1. _____ you got a living room? *Yes,* _____.
2. _____ have they got in the garage? _____ *got a car.*
3. Betty, have _____ got a pretty house? *Yes,* _____.
4. Can you _____ Alan your address? *Yes,* _____.
5. Tom, _____ you show Alan your house? *Yes,* _____.

Make sentences.
1. They, car, bike
2. I, apple, orange
3. You, pen, pencil
4. We, radio, stereo
5. You, chickens, eggs

9•1 Complete the sentences.

1. _____ this? *It's Peter.*
2. _____ this? *It's Mr. and Mrs. Cooper.*
3. It's not raining. _____ go home now.
4. Yes, _____ go. The weather is clearing _____.
5. _____ are the Coopers? _____ *in the bookstore.*
6. _____ are they doing? _____ *buying books.*
7. The guitar is a birthday _____. It's _____ Tom.
8. We _____ buy a newspaper in the bookstore.
9. _____ visit my mother.
10. No, _____. _____ visit my mother.

9•2 Complete the sentences.

1. _____ playing piano? *Helen* _____.
2. _____ Maria and José doing?
   _____ *riding their bicycles.*
3. _____ Betty reading? _____ *reading a newspaper.*
4. _____ eating ice cream? *Maria and Linda* _____.
5. Roland and Tom, what are _____ doing? _____ *watching TV.*
6. Elena, what _____ doing? _____ *looking at photographs.*
7. _____ they doing? _____ *practicing.*
8. _____ practicing? *Tom's band* _____.
9. What _____ are they playing?
   _____ *guitar and piano.*
10. _____ singing? *Helen* _____.

9•3 Read the story.

MR. COOPER: What's this noise? Is it thunder? I can't hear the TV.
PETER: It isn't noise. It isn't thunder. It's music. I'm practicing my drums.
MR. COOPER: Here's money for ice cream, Peter.
PETER: Thank you. But I can't go to the store now. I'm practicing.
MR. COOPER: No, you aren't. You're going to the store. Now!

Answer the questions.

1. What's Peter doing?
2. Can Peter hear thunder?
3. Can Mr. Cooper hear the TV?
4. Where is Peter going?

Unit Eleven

11•1

A. It's here. It's over there.
Where's my sandwich?
It's here.

Where are your jackets?
They're here.

Where's the van?
It's over there.
Where are the tires?
They're over there, too.

Complete the sentences.
■ 1. Where's the van now? *It's here.*
   2. Where are the motorcycles? _____ *here.*
   3. _____ your jacket? _____ *here.*
■ 4. Where's the bus stop? *It's over there.*
   5. Where are the cars? _____ *over there.*
   6. _____ your tires? _____ *over there.*

B. This is a car. That's a van.
This is a car. It's here.
That's a van. It's over there.

Complete the sentences.
■ 1. This is a desk. It's _____. *here*
   2. This is a watch. It's _____.
   3. _____ a notebook. _____ here.
   4. _____ banana. _____ here.
   5. _____ chicken. _____ here.

6. _____ a cookie. _____ over there.
7. _____ an orange. _____ over there.
8. That an egg. It's over _____.
9. That's a clock. It's _____.
10. _____ apple. _____ over there.

C. Where's my book?
ROLAND: Where's my book?
TOM: It's here, on this bed.
ROLAND: No, not this book. This is my old book. Where's my new book?
TOM: It's over there, on that table. Where's my magazine?
ROLAND: Here it is. This is your magazine. It's here, on this chair. Where's my record?
TOM: There it is. That's your record. It's over there, on that shelf.

Identify the speaker. Then answer the questions.
■ 1. _____: Where's my book? *Roland; It's here, on this bed.*
   2. _____: Where's my new book? _____ *on that table.*
   3. _____: Where's my record? _____ *on that shelf.*
   4. _____: Where's my magazine? _____ *on this chair.*

Complete the sentences.
■ 1. Where's Peter's bag? *There it is. That's his bag.*
   2. Where's Linda's record? *Here it is.* _____ *her record.*
   3. Where's my radio? *There it is.* _____ *your radio.*
■ 4. ROLAND: Is this your notebook?
      TOM: No, it isn't. It's Roger's notebook.
         That's my notebook over there.
   5. ROLAND: Is this Betty's notebook?
      TOM: _____, it isn't. This is Peter's notebook.
         That's Betty's notebook _____.
   6. TOM: Is that Alan's motorcycle?
      ROLAND: _____, it is. That's his motorcycle _____.
   7. TOM: Where's the bookstore?
      ROLAND: It's _____ there.
   8. TOM: No, not the old bookstore. Where's the new bookstore?
      ROLAND: It's _____, on this corner.

━━━━━━━━━━━━━━━━━━ *Let's Talk* ━━━━━━━━━━━━━━━━━━

In the store
What are three things you can find in a bookstore? a record store? a drugstore? A classmate is the salesperson.
   Excuse me. Where's the... , please?   *It's over there.*
   Excuse me. Where are the... , please?   *Here are the....*

A. This is interesting. That's boring.

This is a comic book.
It's interesting.
This is an interesting comic book.
This comic book is interesting.

That comic book is boring.
That's a boring comic book.

Complete the sentences. Use *this* and *that*.

■ 1. This is a newspaper. It's big. _____ a big newspaper. *This is*
2. That is a bookstore. It's messy. _____ a messy bookstore.
3. This is a textbook. It's old. _____ an old textbook.
4. That is a shelf. It's long. _____.
5. This is a workbook. It's red. _____.
6. This shoe is clean. _____ shoe is dirty.
7. That umbrella is long. _____ umbrella is short.
8. This van is big. _____ small.
9. That book is interesting. _____.
10. This door is open. _____.

B. There's a broken lamp on the windowsill.

Look at this room. What can you see? *There's a book on the windowsill. There's a lamp on the shelf. It's broken.*

What can't you see in the room? *There's a piano. There are four pictures. There are two chairs. There's one TV.*

Complete and answer the questions.

▪ 1. Is there an organ in the room? *No, there isn't.*
2. Is there a book in the room? *Yes, _____.*
3. Is there a desk?
4. Is there a windowsill?
5. Is there a sofa?
6. Is there a broken lamp?

C. How many are there?

How many rooms are there? *There's one.*
How many pictures are there in the room? *There are four.*

Complete the sentences and answer the questions.

▪ 1. How many chairs are there? *There are two.*
2. How many TV's are there?
3. _____ pianos are there? _____ one.
4. _____ many windows are there? _____ three.
5. _____ lamps _____?

D. Is there a blackboard in the classroom?

This is your classroom at school. What's in the room? There is a teacher. There are a lot of books. There is . . . . There are . . . .

Ask and answer *How many* questions.

▪ 1. Blackboards: How many blackboards are there?
2. Boys: _____?   6. Books: _____?
3. Girls: _____?   7. Teachers: _____?
4. Windows: _____?   8. Desks: _____?
5. Doors: _____?   9. Chairs: _____?

Answer the questions.

1. Is there a teacher in your classroom?
2. Is there a window?   4. Are there two blackboards?
3. Are there a lot of books?   5. Is there a TV?

───────────── *Let's Talk* ─────────────

How many?

How many continents are there?
How many continents in the
northern hemisphere? How many
in the southern? in the eastern?
in the western? How many
poles are there?

How many oceans are there?

A. He's swimming across the river.

What's Alan doing?
*He's swimming across
the river.*

What's Betty doing?
*She's carrying a heavy
box across her room.*

Complete the sentences.

■ 1. What's Linda doing? _____ walking. She's
   She's walking across the street.
   2. What's Tom doing? _____ swimming.
   _____ the lake.
   3. _____ Helen _____?
   She's _____ a small box.
   She's _____ the classroom.

B. It's behind the bus.

Where's the van? *It's behind the bike.*

Complete the sentences.

■ 1. Where's the bike?
   It's in front of _____. the van
   2. Where's the van?
   It's in front of the _____.
   3. Where's the bike?
   It's behind the _____.
   4. Where's the van?
   It's behind the car, and the _____.
   5. Where's the van?
   It's _____ *and* _____.
   6. Where's the bike?
   It's _____ *the van and* _____ *the car.*
   7. Where's the motorcycle?
   It's _____.

C. Play your radio after school.

MR. BROWN: Good morning.

ALL: Good morning, Mr. Brown.

MR. BROWN: What are you doing, Helen?

HELEN: I'm drawing.

MR. BROWN: Very good. But this classroom is a mess.
Let's erase the board.

MARY: Mr. Brown! I can't find my notebook.

MR. BROWN: Is there a notebook on the windowsill, Mary?

MARY: Yes, there is. And it's Betty's.

MR. BROWN: Good. What else is there?

MARY: There are two English books. They're my books.

MR. BROWN: Well, put your books in your desk, Mary.
Betty, what's on your desk? A sweater?

BETTY: Yes, Mr. Brown.

MR. BROWN: You can't write with a sweater on your desk.

BETTY: But, Mr. Brown.

MR. BROWN: Shh. Listen. I can hear music. Is it coming
from your desk, Betty?

BETTY: It's my radio, Mr. Brown. It's under my sweater.

MR. BROWN: Well, please don't play your radio in class.
Play it after school.

Answer *Yes* **or** *No.*
■ 1. The classroom is a mess. *Yes*
  2. Betty's sweater is on her desk.
  3. Mr. Brown can hear music.
  4. Betty's radio is under her desk.
  5. Betty is listening to music.

Complete the sentences. **Use** *windowsill, find, there, classroom, after,*
play.
■ 1. Linda can't ____ her notebook. *find*
  2. The ____ is a mess.
  3. ____ are two English books on the ____ .
  4. ____ your radio ____ class.

Let's Talk

What's where?

Make a floor plan of your room at home. Show the location of everything in the room. Give your plan to a classmate.

  Your bookcase is in the corner, right?   *Yes*

  The window is across from the door, correct?   *No, it's ... .*

  Is your chair behind the ... ?

  Is the ... in front of ... ?

Review

Ask and answer questions.   Here are some examples.

Where's Bill's desk? *It's in front of . . . .*

Where are the tires? *They're . . .*

Vocabulary

Verbs: are carrying, is swimming, is walking

Adjectives: broken, dirty, heavy

Adverbs: here, over, there

Prepositions: across, after

Complete the sentences.   Use the vocabulary above.

1. Where's Bill's notebook? *It isn't here. It's ____.*
2. This is his van. It's ____, in the garage.
3. This car is clean but that car is ____.
4. Don't play your radio now. Play it ____ school.
5. What's Bill doing? *He ____ across the room.*
6. I can't see because the lamp is ____.
7. What's Alan doing? *He ____ across the river.*
8. Betty can't carry the ____ box.
9. The students ____ their books to school.
10. What's Betty doing? *She's running ____ the street.*

Grammar

1. Adverbs
Where's my jacket? *Here* it is. It's *here,* on this chair.
Where's your jacket? *There* it is. It's *over there,* on that chair.

2. Pronouns
This is a car. *That's* a van.

3. Adjectives
This textbook is new. *That* textbook is old.

4. Simple present
Is there a windowsill in the room? Yes, there *is.*
Are there two doors in the room? No, there *aren't.*

5. Question word patterns
How many rooms are there? There's one.
How many pictures are there? There are three.

6. Prepositions
Tom is swimming *across* the river.
Play your radio *after* school.

The car is *behind* the bus.
The bus is *in front of* the van.

Test • Unit 11

11•1 Complete the sentences.

1. Where's your sandwich? _____ *here.*
2. Where's the bus stop? _____ *over there.*
3. _____ your tires? _____ *here.*
4. Where is Tom's room? _____ *it is.* *This is his room.*
5. Where's Linda's record? _____ *it is.* *That's her record.*
6. _____ my sweater? _____ *over there.* *That's your sweater.*
7. _____ Peter's jacket? *It's* _____. *This is his jacket.*

11•2 Complete the sentences.

1. _____ a piano in the living room? _____, *there is.*
2. _____ some cookies in your bag? _____, *there aren't.*
3. _____ a TV in your room? *No,* _____.
4. _____ some apples in the kitchen? *Yes,* _____.
5. That is a jacket. It's red. _____ a red jacket.
6. This is a man. He's angry. _____ an angry man.
7. That's a classroom. It's big. _____ a big classroom.
8. This textbook is new. _____ textbook over there is old.
9. This lamp isn't broken. _____ lamp over there is broken.
10. How many workbooks _____? *There's one.*

11•3 Read the paragraph.

This is Helen's room. It's a large room. There are two beds. There's a big bookcase. There are many books in the bookcase. There's a big desk. There are two lamps on the desk. There are three chairs, and there are many pictures on the walls. There are two windows, and there are blue curtains on the windows.

Answer the questions.

1. Is there a TV in Helen's room?
2. Are there three chairs?
3. How many beds are there?
4. Are there two lamps?
5. Is the desk small?
6. Are there green curtains?
7. How many windows are there?
8. Is there a stereo?
9. Is the room big?
10. Are there many pictures?

110 (one hundred ten)

Maintaining Skills

10•1 Complete the sentences.

1. I have _____ old notebook.
2. This is _____ new sweater.
3. They have _____ carrots.
4. They have _____ cookies.
5. What _____ you have in the box?
6. Do you _____ a chicken?
7. I have a book, but I _____ have a magazine.
8. We _____ a piano, but we don't _____ a guitar.
9. _____ you have some vegetables?
10. What do you _____ in your bag?

10•2 Complete the sentences. Use *are, at, don't, draw, going, on, play, read, ride, sit, to, where's.*

1. No, don't _____ a picture. _____ your book.
2. No, _____ sit on the floor. _____ on a chair.
3. No, don't _____ bikes. _____ your guitars.
4. _____ Linda going? *She's _____ home.*
5. Where's Beth _____? *She's going _____ the corner.*
6. _____ the bus stop? *It's _____ the corner.*
7. Where's John _____? *He's going _____ school.*
8. Where _____ Tom and Alan going? *They _____ going home.*
9. _____ the school? *It's _____ the corner.*
10. Where _____ Peter and Alan playing soccer? *They are playing _____ school.*

10•3 Complete the sentences.

1. Have you got an egg? *Yes, _____.*
2. Peter and Tom, have you got pens? *No, _____.*
3. Tom, _____ I got your book? *Yes, _____.*
4. Betty, _____ you got a watch? *No, _____.*
5. I've got a pen, but I _____ a pencil.
6. _____ have you got in your bag? _____ *got an apple.*
7. _____ you got their address? *No, I _____.*
8. They've got a car, but they _____ a garage.
9. What _____ got in the yard? *They've _____ some flowers.*
10. They've _____ a kitchen, but they haven't got a living room.

Unit Twelve
12•1

A. What's wrong with Linda?

Elena Torres is at home. She's sick. She has a headache. She has a fever. She has a sore throat. She can't talk.

Linda Lee is in the hospital. She's a patient, but she isn't sick. She doesn't have a headache. She doesn't have a sore throat. She doesn't have a fever. What's wrong with Linda? She has a broken leg.

Here are some patients: Ted Johnson, Sally Martin, Michael Peterson, Ann Baker
Here are some ailments: temperature / fever, headache, sore throat, broken leg

Complete the sentences. You choose the ailments.
1. Ted Johnson has a _____.
2. Sally Martin has _____.
3. Michael Peterson _____.
4. Ann Baker _____.

Complete the sentences. Use the ailments above.
■ 1. What's wrong with Elena? *She has a sore throat.*
   2. What's wrong with Linda? *She has a* _____.
   3. What's wrong with Ted? *He has* _____.
   4. _____ wrong with Sally? *She has* _____.
   5. _____ with Ann? *She* _____.
   6. _____ Michael? *He* _____.

Complete the sentences.
■ 1. Elena has a fever, but she _____ a broken leg. *doesn't have*
   2. Linda _____ a broken leg, but she _____ a sore throat.
   3. Ted has a _____, but he doesn't have a _____.
   4. Sally has _____, but she _____.
   5. Michael has _____.

B. Does she have a headache?
Does Linda have a headache? *No, she doesn't.*
Does she have a broken leg? *Yes, she does.*

112 (one hundred twelve)

Complete the sentences and answer the questions.
■ 1. Does Elena have a sore throat? *Yes, she does.*
2. Does Linda have a headache? *No, she* _____.
3. Does Ted have a temperature? *Yes,* _____.
4. Does Ann have a broken leg? *No, she* _____.
5. Does Michael have a sore throat? *No,* _____.
6. Does Sally have a fever?

C. What does Helen have?

Helen is visiting Linda in the hospital. What does she have? *She has a present for Linda. It's a record.* What else does she have? *She has some flowers.*

Complete the sentences and answer the questions.
■ 1. Linda is eating her lunch.
What does she have? *She has a sandwich.*
What else does _____? _____ *an orange.*
What else _____? _____ *a cookie.*
2. Ted is in his room. He's listening to music.
What does he _____? _____ *a radio.*
What else _____? _____ *a lot of magazines.*
What _____? _____ *book.*
3. Does Linda have a sandwich? *Yes, she does.*
_____ she have an apple?
_____ orange?
4. Does Helen have a present? *Yes, she does.*
_____ she have a book?
_____ some flowers?
5. Does Ted have a stereo? *No, he doesn't.*

=========== *Let's Talk* ===========

Call an office.
Mrs. Jones — female, married
Miss Jones — female, single (not married)
Ms. Jones — female, married or single
Mr. Jones — male, married or single
Doctor (Dr.) Jones — male or female, medical doctor

Telephone a classmate's office.
Can I speak to... , please?

This is... .
Yes, please.
My number... .
Good-by.

No, I'm sorry. ...isn't in the office now. Who's calling, please?
Can...call you later?
What's your number?
Thank you.

A. Carlos is feeling sad and Peter is, too.

There's a soccer game at school today. The students are happy. They're playing soccer now.

But Carlos isn't happy. He's feeling sad. He is staying in bed because he has the flu. He is taking his medicine now. He can't play soccer because he's too sick.

Peter is sick, too. He can't smile. He's feeling too ill. His mother is calling up the doctor. She's speaking to the doctor now.

MRS. COOPER: Can I speak to Dr. Jones, please?
DR. JONES: Yes, this is Dr. Jones.
MRS. COOPER: Doctor, this is Mrs. Cooper. My son Peter is sick.
DR. JONES: What's wrong with Peter?
MRS. COOPER: He has red spots on his arms, on his shoulders...
DR. JONES: Does he have red spots all over his body?
MRS. COOPER: Yes, he does.
DR. JONES: Well, that's too bad. He has the measles.
MRS. COOPER: Oh, dear. Can you come and see Peter?
DR. JONES: I'm too busy now, but I can come this afternoon.
MRS. COOPER: Thank you, Doctor. Good-by.

Complete the sentences.
■ 1. Carlos can't play soccer. He's feeling _____ sick. *too*
   2. He can't laugh because he's _____ sad.
   3. Peter can't smile. He feels _____ ill.
   4. The doctor can't come now. He's _____.
   5. The boys aren't happy. They're _____ sick.
   6. That's _____. He has the measles.
   7. Is Carlos feeling happy? *No, _____ sad.*
      Is he eating ice cream? *No, he _____ his medicine.*
   8. Is Peter playing soccer? *No, he _____ in bed.*
      Are his friends reading at school? *No, they _____ soccer.*
   9. Is Mrs. Cooper calling up her friend? *No, she _____ the doctor.*
 10. What's she doing now? *She _____ to the doctor.*

B. Peter doesn't have a cold.

Ailments: a broken leg, a cold, the flu, a headache, the measles, a sore throat, a temperature, fever

Make sentences. You choose the patients.
■ 1. cold: _____. *Linda has a cold.*
     fever: _____. *She doesn't have a fever.*
   2. headache: _____.
     flu: _____.

3. measles: _____.
   temperature: _____.
4. sore throat: _____.
   fever: _____.
5. broken leg: _____.
   measles: _____.

C. The Coopers don't have a van. They have a car.

Luis has an apple. He doesn't have an orange.
The Browns have a yard. They don't have a garage.

Complete the sentences and answer the questions.
■ 1. The Coopers have two sons. _____ three sons. *They don't have*
  2. Linda has a broken leg. _____ a broken arm.
  3. Betty has two brothers. _____ one brother.
  4. Peter has a microphone. _____ telephone.
  5. The Amorosos have a van. _____ car.
  6. What do you have?
  7. What don't you have?

Complete and answer the questions.
■ 1. Does Tom have a motorcycle? *Yes, he does.*
■ 2. Do the Coopers have two cars?
  3. Do the Browns have one car? *Yes, _____.*
  4. Does _____ have a comic book?
  5. Does _____ have a headache?
  6. Do _____ and _____ have a sister?
  7. _____ and _____ have a test today?
  8. _____ have a red sweater?
  9. _____ have a broken arm?
  10. _____ and _____ have notebooks?

Let's Talk

How do you feel?

Greet a classmate. Tell the classmate how you feel.

Hi, ...   Hi. How are you doing?
Oh, not too well. I have a . . . .   Oh, that's too bad.
How about you?   I'm feeling . . . , too.
Oh, that's . . . . I'm sorry.

Hi, ...   Hello. How are you?
I'm feeling great, thanks.   I'm . . . , too.
    And you?

A. Carlos is sick, too.

DR. JONES: Hello, Carlos. What's wrong?

CARLOS: Well, I've got a sore throat, Doctor, and...

DR. JONES: Has he got a temperature?

MRS. AMOROSO: Yes, he has. And his friend Peter has the measles.

DR. JONES: Don't worry. Carlos hasn't got spots.

CARLOS: But I've got a headache.

MRS. AMOROSO: What has he got, Doctor?

DR. JONES: Well, let's see. Open your mouth, Carlos.

MRS. AMOROSO: Has he got a cold again, Doctor?

DR. JONES: No, he doesn't. This time he's got the flu.

CARLOS: Can I go to school today, Dr. Jones? I am having an English test today.

DR. JONES: No, you can't.

CARLOS: Can I go tomorrow? There's a big soccer game tomorrow.

DR. JONES: Too bad, Carlos. Stay in bed for three days and take this medicine.

CARLOS: Three days in bed! Oh, no!

DR. JONES: Oh, yes! Three days. Well, good-by, Carlos. Good-by, Mrs. Amoroso.

MRS. AMOROSO: Good-by, Doctor.

Answer the questions.

■ 1. What's wrong with Carlos? *He's got a sore throat and a temperature.*
  2. Has he got the measles?
  3. Has Peter got the measles?
  4. Has Carlos got a headache?
  5. Has he got a cold again?
  6. Has he got the flu?
  7. Can he go to school today?
  8. Has he got a test today?

Complete the sentences.

■ 1. What ＿＿＿ he got, Doctor? *has*
     Well, let's see. Open your ＿＿＿, Peter.
     He hasn't ＿＿＿ the flu this time.
  2. ＿＿＿ I go to school today, Doctor?
     No, ＿＿＿ in bed for three days and ＿＿＿ this medicine.

B. Dr. Jones is writing a textbook.

Here is a picture for her book:

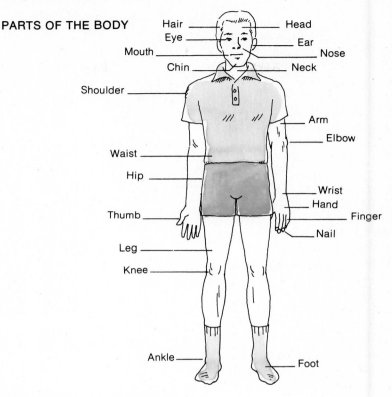

PARTS OF THE BODY

Hair — Head
Eye — Ear
Mouth — Nose
Chin — Neck
Shoulder —
Arm —
Elbow —
Waist —
Hip —
Wrist —
Hand —
Thumb — Finger
Nail —
Leg —
Knee —
Ankle — Foot

Draw the pictures.   Label the parts.
1. Draw a picture of an arm.   Label the elbow, the wrist, and the hand.
2. Draw a picture of a hand.   Label the fingers, the thumb, and the nails.
3. Draw a picture of a leg.   Label the knee, the ankle, and the foot.
4. Draw a picture of a head.   Label the hair, the eyes, the nose, the ears, the mouth, and the chin.

Let's Talk

In the Doctor's Office

You are the doctor.   A classmate is sick.   Find out what's wrong and tell that classmate what to do.

Hello, ...   What's wrong?   *Doctor, I'm not feeling well.*
That's too bad.
Let's take your temperature.   *Do I have a fever?*
Yes, you do.
Do you have a sore throat?   *No, but . . . .*
Here's your medicine.   *Thanks, Doctor . . . .*

Grammar: Items 1 and 2   (one hundred seventeen) **117**

Review

Describe the activity in the picture. Here are some examples.

What's wrong? *My arm is broken.*
What else is wrong? *I have a headache.*
Can I call your family? What's the number?

Vocabulary

Nouns: doctor, flu, leg, spots, temperature
Verbs: are speaking, is staying, is taking
Adjectives: sad, sore

Complete the sentences. Use the vocabulary above.

1. Peter is sick. Mrs. Cooper is calling up the _____.
2. Linda isn't happy. She's _____.
3. Mr. Cooper is sick. He has a _____ throat.
4. Peter has the measles. He has _____ all over his body.
5. Mrs. Cooper is feeling sick. She _____ in bed today.
6. Carlos is sick, too. He _____ his medicine now.
7. Is this Dr. Jones? *Yes, you _____ to Dr. Jones.*
8. Helen has a _____ and a headache.
9. Mrs. Lee is sad. Linda has a broken _____.
10. Tom is feeling sick. He has the _____ again.

118 (one hundred eighteen)

1. **Simple present**
   Elena *has* a temperature.
   Does she *have* a sore throat?   Yes, she *does*.
   Linda *has* a broken leg, but she *doesn't have* a fever.
   Does she *have* a cold?   No, she *doesn't*.

   Sally *has got* the flu, but she *hasn't got* a fever.
   Has she *got* a broken leg?   No, she *hasn't*.

2. **Question word patterns**
   What does Linda have?   She has a broken leg.
   What has Sally got?   She has a headache.

3. **Present progressive**
   Carlos *is feeling* sick.

4. **Adverbs**
   He can't play soccer.   He's *too* sick.

5. **Articles**
   Ann Baker has *the* flu.   She doesn't have *a* cold.

12•1 Complete the sentences.

1. Peter is sick. He _____ a temperature.
2. Sally has a headache but she _____ have a fever.
3. Does Linda _____ a broken leg? *Yes, _____.*
4. Linda has a clock _____ she doesn't have a watch.
   _____ she have a radio? *Yes, _____.*
5. _____ wrong with Mr. Brown? *He _____ a cold.*
6. _____ does Betty have in her bag?
   She _____ three new magazines.

12•2 Complete the sentences.

1. Elena _____ in bed because she _____ the flu.
2. Her mouth is open. She _____ her medicine.
3. Peter has _____ measles.
4. The Coopers have a car. They _____ have a van.
5. Tom _____ a radio but he doesn't _____ a record player.
6. Sally has _____ sore throat.
7. Tom has a headache. He _____ sick.
8. Mrs. Cooper _____ the doctor.
9. Betty _____ to Helen on the telephone.
10. Do the Coopers have a TV? *Yes, they _____.*
11. _____ Carlos and Peter have the flu? *No, they _____.*
12. _____ Elena have a bad cold? *No, she _____.*
13. _____ Tom have a *new* motorcycle? *No, he _____.*

12•3 Read the story.

   Mr. Cooper is staying in bed. He hasn't got a cold or the flu. He has got a sore leg. He can't go to work and he can't go outside. He's reading a book and listening to the radio. He doesn't have a television in his room. He's bored.

Answer the questions.

1. What's wrong with Mr. Cooper?
2. Has he got a cold, too?
3. Where is he staying?
4. Can he go to work?
5. Is he reading a book?
6. What else is he doing?
7. Does he have a television?
8. Is he happy?

11•1 Complete the sentences. Use *this* or *that*.

1. LINDA: Is this your bike?
   BETTY: No, it isn't. It's Helen's bike. _____ is my bike over there.
2. CARLOS: Where are my shoes?
   PETER: Here they are. They're on _____ table.
3. HELEN: Is _____ your jacket over there?
   TOM: No. My jacket is blue. _____ jacket is grey.
4. MRS. COOPER: Where's my shopping bag?
   MR. COOPER: It's here, in _____ closet.

11•2 Complete the sentences.

1. This lamp is broken. This is a _____ lamp.
2. That bike is old. That's an _____ bike.
3. This window is dirty. This is a _____ window.
4. That box is small. That's a _____ box.
5. There _____ eleven chairs in the room.
6. There _____ one window.
7. _____ there five workbooks here? *No, there _____.*
8. _____ there a bike over there? *Yes, there _____.*
9. _____ there a radio on the windowsill? *No, there _____.*
10. Are _____ ten boys in this class? *Yes, _____ are.*
11. How many vans _____ there in the garage? *There _____ two.*
12. _____ there two radios in your van? *No, there _____.*

Extra!

What's wrong? Change the letters in the wrong word.

1. He has red stops all over his body.
2. How's this? *It's Mr. and Mrs. Cooper.*
3. The record is on the pot shelf.
4. Can you count from one to net?
5. I can see her sobs.
6. Is Tom swimming in the kale?
7. She can't see. Her palm is broken.
8. Carlos is the first. Peter is the salt.
9. My mar is on his shoulder.
10. Can she see your miles?

Unit Thirteen

13•1

A. Frank has to wash his hands.

Frank Allen is a gardener.
He works in the garden.
His hands are dirty.
He has to wash his hands.
His arms are dirty.
He has to wash his arms.

Rita Jones is a doctor.
She works in the hospital.
Her hands are clean now.
She doesn't have to wash her arms.

Complete the sentences. Use *has to* or *doesn't have to.*
- 1. The truck is dirty. Mr. Allen _____ wash his truck. *has to*
  2. It's raining. The truck is clean now. Mr. Allen _____ wash his truck.
  3. Doctor (Dr.) Jones has a broken lamp. She _____ buy a new lamp.
  4. Mr. Allen's radio is broken, but he can fix the radio. He _____ buy a new radio.
  5. The woman is sick. She _____ stay in bed today.
  6. Mr. Allen isn't sick now. He _____ work today.

B. Do you have to take medicine? Yes, I do.

You aren't sick, Mr. and Mrs. Allen. Do you have to take medicine?
No, we don't.

The Allens have a new car. Do they have to take the bus?
No, they don't.

Complete and answer the questions.
- 1. You're sick.
   Do you have to take medicine? *Yes, I do.*
  2. Mr. Allen's hands are dirty.
   Does he have to wash his hands?
  3. The windows in the truck are clean.
   _____ Mr. Allen have to wash the windows?
  4. I am having an English test today.
   _____ I have to go to school?

5. I'm sick today.
   Do I _____ go to school today?
6. You have to give a test tomorrow, Dr. Jones.
   Do the students _____ read your book?
7. Dr. Jones can take the bus to the hospital.
   _____ have to walk?
8. Mr. Allen's shoes are dirty.
   _____ clean his shoes?

C. What do you have to do?

What do you have to do? *I have to buy lunch.*
What does he have to do? *He has to leave now.*
What do you have to do? *We have to listen.*
What do they have to do? *They have to practice.*

Complete the sentences.
■ 1. What does Peter have to do? *He has to clean his room.*
  2. _____ does Betty have to do?
     _____ *take a class.*
  3. _____ do Tom and Roland have to do?
     _____ *practice.*
  4. _____ you have to do, Mrs. Cooper?
     _____ *help Peter.*
  5. _____ Mr. Cooper _____ do?
     _____ *call up the doctor.*
  6. _____ Dr. Jones have to _____?
     _____ *visit Peter.*
  7. _____ Peter _____?
     _____ *his medicine.*
     Now Peter doesn't have to clean his room.   He's too sick.

Answer the questions.
  1. What do you have to do now?
  2. What do you have to do after class?
  3. What do you have to do first?
  4. What do you have to do last?

═══════════ Let's Talk ═══════════

Make and refuse invitations.

Invite your classmate to your house. Your classmate has to refuse the
invitation (say no).
   Can you come to my house?   *I'm sorry. I can't. I have to . . . .*
Invite your classmate again.
   Can you go to lunch?   *No, I'm very sorry. I . . . .*
   Can you go to the park?

A. Whose living room is this?

Whose cup is this?
It's Mrs. Cooper's.
Whose tennis rackets
are these?
They're Tom's.

Complete and answer the questions.

■ 1. Whose soccer shoes are these? *They're Peter's.*
2. Whose umbrella is this? _____ *Betty's.*
3. _____ newspaper is this? _____ *Mrs. Cooper's.*
4. _____ tennis racket is this?
5. _____ purse is this?
6. _____ sweater _____?
7. _____ book _____?
8. _____ raincoat _____?

B. It's a rainy day.

Mrs. Cooper is looking out the window. She can see five people at the bus stop, three men and two women. They have to stand in the rain.

Peter is reading his friend's book. He's laughing because it's very funny.

Mary and Betty are studying. They have to take a test. They're learning to drive. Betty is asking the questions. Mary is answering.

Tom is listening to his records. He has to find new music for the band. Roland and Tom have to practice this afternoon.

Answer the questions.
- 1. Is the weather good or bad today? *It's bad.*
- 2. What's Mrs. Cooper doing? *She's looking out the window.*
  3. What's Peter doing now?
     Is it his book?
     Whose book is it?
  4. What are Mary and Betty doing?
     What is Betty doing?
     Are they Betty's answers?
  5. What is Tom doing?
     What does he have to do?
     Are they Tom's records?

Match the answers with the questions. Use the letters.

- 1. Is Peter playing soccer?
  2. Is it Peter's book?
  3. Whose book is it?
  4. Are they Betty's answers?
  5. Whose answers are they?

    a. No, they aren't.
    b. No, he isn't.
    c. They're Mary's.
    d. No, it isn't.
    e. It's his friend's.

Let's Talk

Give directions.

Drive to the bookstore. Go straight (↑) for three blocks. Turn right (↱). Take the fourth left (↰). Go straight for three more blocks.

Your classmates are driving to the music store. Give directions. Vary the directions.
    Go...for....

				Book Store

Music Store

Start Here

A. A Telephone Call

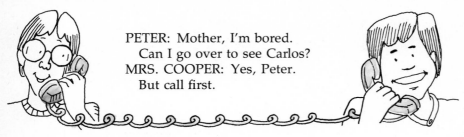

PETER: Mother, I'm bored.
Can I go over to see Carlos?
MRS. COOPER: Yes, Peter.
But call first.

PETER: Hi, Carlos! How are you feeling today?
CARLOS: Oh, I'm O.K. I don't have to stay in bed today.
How are you?
PETER: I'm feeling fine now. I can go outside today.
CARLOS: I can't. I have to stay inside. Doctor's orders.
PETER: That's too bad. What's wrong with you?
Can you have visitors?
CARLOS: Sure I can. Can you come over?
PETER: Wait a minute. I can ask my mother.... I can come over,
Carlos. What are you doing?
CARLOS: I'm reading a book because I'm learning English. It's a funny
book. But it's not my book.
PETER: Whose book is it?
CARLOS: It's Mr. Brown's.
PETER: Oh, well. I'm coming over right now.
CARLOS: O.K. Can I borrow your records?
PETER: Records? Sure, I can bring some records. What else?
CARLOS: Some games.
PETER: O.K. I'm leaving right now.

Answer *Yes* or *No*.
■ 1. Peter is calling up Carlos. *Yes*
2. Carlos can go outside.
3. Peter can go over to Carlos right now.
4. Carlos can borrow Peter's records.

Answer the questions.
■ 1. How is Carlos feeling today? *He's feeling O.K.*
2. Is Peter feeling O.K., too?
3. Can Peter go outside today?
4. Does Carlos have to stay inside?
5. What's Carlos borrowing?
6. Is Peter going over right now?

B. Peter can lend Carlos his records.

Mr. Brown is teaching English.
Carlos is learning English.

Peter is lending the records.
Carlos is borrowing the records.

Peter is giving the records.
Carlos is receiving the records.

Complete the sentences.
■ 1. PETER: Mother, I'm ____ to see Carlos. *going over*
    CARLOS: Peter, ____ to my house? *are you coming over*
  2. I ____ Carlos the records.
    Carlos ____ the records.
  3. Mr. Brown ____ English.
    The students ____ English.
  4. I ____ Tom a present.
    Tom ____ the present.
  5. I ____ the money from you.
    You ____ the money.

C. Peter and Carlos are drawing.

Carlos is drawing Peter.
Peter is drawing a robot.

Complete the sentences.
■ 1. CARLOS: You ____ have a head. *have to*
    PETER: It can have a head.
  2. CARLOS: You ____ two eyes.
    PETER: It ____ one eye.
  3. PETER: It ____ one foot.
    CARLOS: You ____ two feet.
  4. PETER: It doesn't have to have a tooth.
    CARLOS: You have ____ teeth.

Let's Talk

Where is the restroom?

Ask a classmate where these things are: the door, the post office, his or her house, the restroom.

  Excuse me, where is... ?   *I'm sorry. I can't tell you.*
  Where's the... ?   *It's... .*

Review

What do they have to do? Here are some examples.

This is Frank.... He's.... He has to....
This is.... She's.... She doesn't have to....

Vocabulary

   Nouns: cup, raincoat
   Verbs: borrow, go, lend, study, teach, wash
   Adverbs: sure
   Adjectives: funny, rainy, whose

Complete the sentences. Use the vocabulary above.

  1. Tom's motorcycle is dirty. He has to _____ the motorcycle today.
  2. I can see five _____ on the table.
  3. Can you come over to my house? Mother, can I _____ over to see Carlos?
  4. Peter's laughing because the book is _____.
  5. Can you _____ Tom the money?
  6. Tom has a lot of money. He doesn't have to _____ the money.
  7. It's a _____ day. Peter can't go outside.
  8. _____ tennis rackets are these? *They're Tom's.*
  9. Can you come over to my house? _____, *I'm coming over now.*
 10. What are Helen and Linda doing? *They're* _____.
 11. Mr. Brown _____ the students.
 12. Helen is taking her _____ because it's raining.

Grammar

1. **Modals**
   I am sick.   I *have to* stay in bed.
   You *have to* stay inside.
   He *has to* wash his hands.
   She *doesn't have to* wash her hands.
   They *don't have to* stay inside.

   Do you *have to* study?   Yes, we *do.*
   Does she *have to* take the bus?   No, she *doesn't.*

   A man or woman *has to have* a head.
   A robot *doesn't have to have* a head.

2. **Question word patterns**
   What do you have to do?   I have to take my medicine.
   What does your friend have to do?   He has to study.

   Whose cup is this?   It's Mrs. Cooper's.
   Whose is this?   It's Peter's.
   Whose tennis rackets are these?   They're Tom's.
   Whose are these?   They're Betty's.

3. **Nouns**
   man   woman
   men   women

   tooth
   teeth

4. **Verbs**
   CARLOS: Can you *come over* to my house, Peter?
   PETER: Mother, can I *go over* to see Carlos?
   PETER: Yes, Carlos.   I can *come over.*

   Mr. Brown is *teaching* English.
   Carlos is *learning* English.

   Peter is *lending* Carlos the records.
   Carlos is *borrowing* the records.

   Peter is *giving* the records.
   Carlos is *receiving* the records.

13•1   Complete the sentences.

1. Her hair is dirty.   She _____ wash her hair.
2. It's raining.   We _____ stay home.
3. Tom isn't sick.   He _____ stay inside.
4. _____ you have to work today?   *No, I _____.*
5. What do you _____ do?   _____ *wash my hair.*
6. _____ Peter _____ fix his bike?   *Yes, he _____.*
7. The car is clean.   I _____ wash it.
8. The radio is broken.   Tom _____ fix it.
9. Roland has a test tomorrow.   What _____ he _____ do?
   He _____ read his English book.

13•2   Complete and answer the questions.

1. _____ microphone is this?   _____ *Helen's.*
2. _____ trees _____ these?   _____ *Mr. Allen's.*
3. _____ tennis rackets are these?   _____ *Tom's.*
4. _____ these Mary's answers?   *Yes, _____.*
5. _____ they Betty's answers?   *No, _____.*
6. _____ jackets are these?   _____ *Peter's and Tom's.*
7. _____ jacket is this?   _____ *Peter's.*

13•3   Complete the sentences.   Use *lend, borrow; give, receive; teach, learn; come, go.*

1. Peter has to buy a record.
   Tom can _____ Peter the money.
   Peter can _____ the money.
2. Mr. Brown is a teacher.   He _____ English now.
   Carlos is a student.   He _____ English now.
3. Carlos, can you _____ over to my house?
   Mother, can I _____ to see Carlos?
4. Betty _____ Helen a present now.
   Helen _____ the present.

Complete the sentences.
1. A robot can have one tooth.
   A man or woman has to have many _____.
2. A robot can have one foot.
   A man or woman has to have two _____.

12•1 Complete the sentences.

1. Elena is sick.   She _____ a sore throat.
2. Tom isn't sick.   He _____ a fever.
3. Does Linda _____ a broken leg?   *Yes,* _____.
4. What _____ Mrs. Cooper _____?   *She* _____ *a radio.*
5. _____ Mr. Cooper have a temperature?   *No,* _____.
6. Mr. Cooper _____ a sore throat but he _____ have a fever.
7. What's _____ with Tom now?   *He* _____ *a headache.*
8. _____ Roland have his guitar?   *No,* _____.

12•2 Complete the sentences.

1. Roland is _____ sick.
2. His mother is _____ up the doctor.
3. Roland's mouth is open.   He's _____ his medicine.
4. They have a house but they _____ a garage.
5. Tom doesn't _____ a sore throat.   He _____ a cold.
6. _____ the Coopers have two cars?
   No, _____.   _____ *one car.*
7. Tom and Roland _____ guitars.
   _____ they _____ drums, too?   *Yes,* _____.
8. Does Tom _____ a stereo?   *Yes,* _____.

12•3 Read the story.

   Roland isn't feeling well today.   He's staying in bed.   He has a temperature and a sore throat.   He can't go to the music store.   He can't work today.
   Roland is calling up the doctor on the telephone.   He's talking to the doctor about his temperature and sore throat.   He is going to the doctor's this afternoon.   The doctor has medicine for Roland's temperature.

Answer the questions.
1. Is Roland feeling well today?
2. What's wrong with Roland?
3. Can he work today?
4. What is Roland doing?
5. What does the doctor have for Roland?

Unit Fourteen
14•1

A. Plurals
The sound of the plural is / s / or / z /.

suit
suits / s /

necktie
neckties / z /

The sound of the plural is / ɪz /

blouse
blouses / ɪz /

dress
dresses / ɪz /

watch — watches / ɪz /   box — boxes / ɪz /
bush — bushes / ɪz /   nose — noses / ɪz /
cage — cages / ɪz /

Complete the sentences.
■ 1. This is a bench. _____ are benches. *These*
   2. _____ a cage. These are _____.
   3. _____ a box. These _____.
   4. _____ orange. These _____.
   5. _____ nose. _____.
   6. _____ dress. _____.
   7. _____ blouse. _____.
   8. _____ bush. _____.

B. Linda has two pairs of slippers.
She has two pairs of white slippers.
She has one pair of white socks.
She has a pair of white gloves, too.

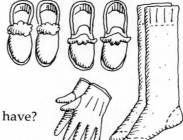

Complete the sentences.
■ 1. How many pairs of slippers does Linda have?
   She has _____ *pairs of slippers.* *two*
   2. How many _____ of gloves does Linda have?
   She has one _____.
   3. _____ of white socks does she have?
   She has one pair of white socks.

C. Whose shorts are they?

This is a pair of shorts.
Whose shorts are they?
They're Tom's.

Complete the sentences.

- 1. This is a pair of jeans.
     Whose _____ are they? *jeans*
     They're Tom's, too.
  2. This is a pair of shoes.
     Whose _____ are they?
     _____ Alan's.
  3. This is a pair of socks.
     _____ are they?
     _____ Tom's.

D. Tom is packing his suitcase.

Look at Tom's suitcase.
He's packing his things.
There are jeans, shorts,
sneakers, and socks.

Complete the sentences.

- 1. There are _____ of jeans. *two pairs*
  2. _____ three _____.
  3. _____ four _____.
  4. There is _____ sneakers.

Let's Talk

Find the owner.

Your classmates are leaving your house after a party. They can't find
some things: coats, sweaters, purses, car keys, house keys.

    This isn't my . . . .
Whose . . . is this?   *It's . . . .*
Whose . . . are these?   *They're . . . .*
Where's my . . . ?

A. Those are boots.

 This is
a belt.

That's a
belt, too.

 These
are boots.

Those are
boots, too.

Complete the sentences.

■ 1. _____ are my belts. They're here. *These*
2. _____ are my records. They're over there.
3. _____ is my telephone. It's here.
4. _____ are my slippers. They're over there.
5. _____ my gloves. _____ here.
6. _____ my suitcase. _____ over there.
7. These are my sneakers. _____.
8. That's my blouse. _____.
9. This is my sister. _____.
10. Those are my brothers. _____.
11. _____ is my _____. He's _____.
12. _____ are my _____. _____.

B. The other pair is Tom's.

Where are the scissors?
One pair is on the table.
The other pair is on
the floor.

Whose pants are they?
One pair is Betty's.
The other pair is Tom's.

Who's wearing a pair
of glasses?
The tailor is.
Where are the vests?
One is in the window.
The other is in his hands.

Complete the sentences.

■ 1. _____ pants are those? *Whose*
_____ *is Helen's and* _____ *is Betty's.*
2. _____ vests are those?
_____ *is Peter's and* _____ *is his father's.*
3. _____ blouses are those?
_____ *Mary's and* _____ *Elena's.*
4. _____ jeans _____?
_____ *Tom's and* _____ *Alan's.*
5. _____ dresses _____?
_____ *Linda's and* _____ *Helen's.*
6. _____ socks _____?
_____ *Roger's and* _____ *Roland's.*
7. _____ slippers _____?
_____ .
8. _____ jeans _____?
_____ .

Complete the sentences. You have two pairs of these things. You can vary the answers.

1. Where are your shoes?
One pair is _____. *The other pair is* _____.
2. Where are your jeans?
One pair is _____. *The other pair is* _____.
3. Where are your socks?
One pair is _____. *The other pair is* _____.
4. Where are your glasses?
One _____. *The* _____.
5. Where are your scissors?
6. Where are your slippers?
7. Where are your tennis shorts?

━━━━━━━━━━ Let's Talk ━━━━━━━━━━

How many pairs?
How many classmates have blue eyes?
How many pairs of classmates have blue eyes?
How many pairs of classmates have brown eyes?
How many pairs of classmates wear glasses?
How many pairs of classmates wear glasses
    and have brown hair?
How many pairs of classmates can drive?
How many classmates eat sandwiches?
How many pairs of... ?

Grammar: Items 3 and 4   (one hundred thirty-five) **135**

A. What's going on?

Mary and Betty are jogging. Betty's sneaker is coming off. Now she's putting on her sneaker again. It's cloudy and windy now. Mary is taking off her sunglasses. She's waiting for Betty.

Verbs and Prepositions

		Two-word verbs:	
come over	look in		call up
go into	look on		clear up
go out of	look out		go on
go over	stand on		put on
look at	wait for		take off

Complete the sentences. Use the verbs above.

■ 1. MARY: Betty, it's too windy now.
        Can you _____ to my house? *come over*
2. BETTY: I can't, Mary. I'm _____ to Linda's.
3. MARY: Can I come, too? I can _____ Linda.
4. BETTY: O.K. Let's _____ the park.
5. Linda is at home. She's _____ Betty and Mary.
6. Now Betty and Mary are _____ Linda's house.
7. LINDA: Betty and Mary, _____ your jackets.
8. BETTY: Linda, what's _____?
9. LINDA: Get into the living room. _____ my new piano.
10. Mrs. Lee is _____ the window. She has to leave now.
11. It's raining. She has to _____ a rain hat.
12. Where's the hat? Mrs. Lee is _____ the closet.
13. She's _____ the top shelf. Is her rain hat there?
14. She's short. She has to _____ a chair.
15. LINDA: Mother, the weather is _____ now.

B. It's a surprise.

BETTY: Peter, what are you doing?

PETER: I'm doing the wash. It's a surprise for mother.

BETTY: Oh, can you wash my brown jogging clothes?

PETER: Let's see. What's in the washing machine now? I've got three white blouses, mother's two new dresses, four very dirty shirts, some white socks, and a pair of shorts.

BETTY: There's room.

PETER: O.K., put your clothes in the machine.

BETTY: Thanks, Peter.

PETER: Hi, mother. Oh, what a heavy bag! Sit down.

MRS. COOPER: Gladly. I'm wearing a new pair of shoes. Oh, my feet! I have to take off these shoes. Hey, what's that noise?

PETER: Noise? Oh, it's the washing machine. It's a surprise.

MRS. COOPER: A surprise?

PETER: Yes, the dirty clothes are in the machine.

MRS. COOPER: All the dirty clothes?

PETER: Right. Look in the machine.

MRS. COOPER: Oh, no!

PETER: What's wrong?

MRS. COOPER: Look at the colors! Whose blouses are these? Whose dresses are these? Everything is brown!

PETER: Brown? Oh-oh, brown. Well, uh, that's the other surprise.

Answer the questions.

■ 1. What is Peter doing? *He's doing the wash.*
   2. Is there room in the washing machine for Betty's brown jogging clothes?
   3. What is Mrs. Cooper carrying?
   4. What is Mrs. Cooper taking off?
   5. Where are the dirty clothes?
   6. What color are the clothes in the washing machine?
   7. Is Mrs. Cooper happy about the brown clothes?

Let's Talk

What are you wearing?

Your classmate is jogging. It's cold. Ask what he or she is wearing.

   What are you wearing?   *I'm . . . .*
   What else?   *A pair of . . . .*

Continue with swimming, tennis, and soccer.

You're having a party. What are you wearing?

Review

Ask and answer questions.

Tom is at the airport. He is taking an airplane. Where is he going? Why is he going there? What does he have in his suitcase? How many questions can you ask? How many answers can your classmates give?

Vocabulary

Nouns: clothes, pair, room, slippers, surprise, vest, wash, washing machine

Verbs: putting on, taking off

Complete the sentences. Use the vocabulary above.

1. Betty isn't wearing shoes. She's wearing _____ .
2. Mrs. Cooper is washing the clothes in the _____ .
3. Is there _____ for my blouse in the washing machine?
4. I have a _____ of jeans, but I don't have a dress.
5. Peter is putting the dirty _____ in the washing machine.
6. Mrs. Cooper isn't feeling well. Betty is doing the _____ today.
7. Tom's suit has a _____ .
8. Peter is _____ his dirty shirt.
9. PETER: I'm cleaning my room. It's a _____ for Mom.
10. Mrs. Cooper is taking off her shoes. She's _____ her slippers.

Grammar

1. **Nouns**
   bus — bus*es* / ɪz /
   nose — nos*es* / ɪz /
   cage — cag*es* / ɪz /
   watch — watch*es* / ɪz /
   bush — bush*es* / ɪz /
   box — box*es* / ɪz /

   Tom has a *pair of* shorts.   Linda has a *pair of* slippers.
   He has two *pairs of* jeans.   She has two *pairs of* shoes.

2. **Pronouns**
   This is a boot.   *That* is a slipper.
   These are suits.   *Those* are dresses.
   This is a blouse.   *That's* a belt.
   These are glasses.   *Those* are scissors.

3. **Adjectives**   **Pronouns**
   One pair of pants is on the chair.   *One* is on the chair.
   The *other* pair of pants is on the bed.   The *other* is on the bed.

4. **Two-word verbs**
   What's *going on*?
   Mrs. Cooper is *taking off* her shoes.
   Now she is *putting on* her slippers.

5. **Verbs and Prepositions**
   Look on the shelf. Is my radio there?
   Look at the book. Can you see her picture?
   Look out the window. It's raining.
   Look in the box. It's a new pair of gloves.

14•1 Complete the sentences. Use the plural form of the word in italics.

1. Mr. Allen's yard has one *bush*. My yard has four _____.
2. Betty has one *box*, but I have two _____.
3. Linda is packing one *dress*. Helen is packing three _____.
4. Mrs. Cooper has one new *blouse*. Betty has two new _____.
5. José's school has one *bus*. Peter's school has three _____.

Complete the sentences. Use *pair of* or *pairs of*.
6. I have one _____ new shoes and two _____ old shoes.
7. How many _____ shorts do you have?
8. I have four _____ slippers.
9. How many _____ jeans does Helen have?
   She has one _____ jeans and two _____ shorts.

14•2 Complete the sentences. Use *that* or *those*.

1. _____ jeans are Tom's.
2. Is _____ sweater new?
3. _____ dress is big.
4. Are _____ shoes old?
5. _____ blouse is on the chair.
6. Whose shorts are _____?

14•3 Read the story.

  Peter is helping his mother today. He's doing the wash. He is standing in front of the washing machine. He's putting dirty clothes into the machine. Tom's vest and a pair of jeans are in the machine. There's a pair of Betty's socks, too.
  Peter's mother is outside in the yard. She's working in the garden. She's happy because Peter is helping today.

Answer *Yes* or *No*.
1. Peter is outside.
2. Peter's mother is doing the wash.
3. Betty's vest is in the machine.
4. There's a pair of jeans in the machine.
5. The clothes are outside in the yard.
6. Peter's mother is sad today.

Complete the sentences.
7. Tom can see the game outside. He's looking _____ the window.
8. Betty is late. Mary is waiting _____ Betty.
9. She's taking _____ her old shoes. She's putting _____ the new shoes.

13•1 Complete the sentences.

1. Tom _____ to go to school but he _____ to work at the store.
2. What _____ Linda _____ do?
3. *She _____ practice the piano.*
4. _____ you _____ to clean your room? *No, _____.*
5. The gardener's hands are dirty. He _____ wash his hands.
6. I'm sick. I _____ stay home.
7. What _____ they _____ to do? *They _____ practice.*
8. _____ Tom _____ wash the window? *No, _____.*

13•2 Complete the sentences.

1. _____ cup is this? _____ *Mrs. Cooper's.*
2. _____ this? _____ *Peter.*
3. _____ tennis rackets are these? _____ *Tom's.*
4. _____ this? _____ *Betty and Linda.*
5. _____ records are they? _____ *Roland's.*
6. _____ this Tom's jacket? *Yes, _____.*
7. _____ Tom and Betty playing music? *No, _____.*
8. _____ it Peter's? *No, _____ Mr. Brown's.*
9. _____ are Linda and Betty doing? _____ *studying.*
10. _____ asking questions? *Betty _____.*

13•3 Read the story.

Tom has to work today. His boss is sick. She can't work. She has to stay home. Tom is happy because he doesn't have to work tomorrow. And today he is the boss!

Answer the questions.
1. What does Tom have to do today?
2. What's wrong with his boss?
3. Can she work today?
4. Does she have to stay home?
5. Does Tom have to work tomorrow?
6. Is Tom the boss today?

Unit Fifteen

15•1

A. Are there any jeans?

You're at the shopping mall. You're standing in front of a depart-ment store. You're window-shopping. You're looking at the clothes and the prices. There are some blouses, some skirts, and some boots in the window. There's a dress, too. There's a pair of jeans, but there aren't any shorts.

Are there any shoes? There are some socks, but there aren't any shoes.

Complete the sentences. Answer the questions.

■ 1. Are there any jeans in the window? *Yes, there are.*
2. Are there any shoes? *No, _____.*
3. _____ any blouses? *Yes, _____.*
4. _____ any shirts? *No, _____.*
5. _____ dresses? *Yes, _____ one.*
6. _____ coats?
7. _____ hats?
8. _____ some blouses, but there aren't any shirts
9. _____ some boots, but there _____ shoes.
10. _____ any coats, but _____ some boots.
11. _____ hats, but _____ jeans.
12. _____ shoes, but _____ socks.

B. Numbers and U.S. monetary units

21	twenty-one	31	thirty-one	60	sixty
22	twenty-two	39	thirty-nine	70	seventy
23	twenty-three	40	forty	80	eighty
29	twenty-nine	41	forty-one	90	ninety
30	thirty	50	fifty	100	one hundred

101	one hundred one		1000	one thousand
121	one hundred twenty-one		1001	one thousand one

One U.S. dollar
$1.00
100¢

penny $.01   nickel $.05   dime $.10   quarter $.25
  1¢   5¢   10¢   25¢

Complete the sentences and answer the questions. Use the prices on page 142.

■ 1. How much is the dress? *It's eighty-nine ninety-five; $89.95.*
   2. How much ___ the socks? *They're ___.*
   3. ___ the blouses?
   4. ___ the jeans?
   5. ___ your textbook?

Let's Talk

How much?

You're shopping. Ask the salesperson the price of things.

How much is this?	*It's $25.00.*
$25.00? That's too expensive.	*How about this?*
How much is that?	*It's . . . .*
That's very expensive, too.	*But . . . .*
O.K. Here's the money.	*Thank you.*

Grammar: Items 1 and 2

(one hundred forty-three) **143**

A. They are all going shopping.

Mrs. Cooper, Betty, and Peter are going shopping at the mall. They have to buy some new things. Betty has to buy a new pair of boots. Mrs. Cooper has to buy a dress. She has to buy some socks for Peter. Peter has to buy a present for his father.

Answer *That's right* **or** *That's wrong.*

■ 1. They're going shopping at the mall. *That's right.*
2. Mrs. Cooper has to buy a sweater.
3. Peter has to buy a present for his mother.
4. Mrs. Cooper has to buy some socks for Tom.
5. Betty has to buy some new boots.

B. These boots are so pretty.

Mrs. Cooper, Betty, and Peter are now in the shoe department. Betty is trying on boots and talking to her mother. All the boots are so expensive. They're $100.00 a pair. Are they too expensive? Let's see.

BETTY: This pair is too big. That pair is too small. This pair is
  just right. They're so pretty, but they're so expensive.
MRS. COOPER: That's all right, Betty. I can lend you some money.
BETTY: Oh, I'm so happy, mother. Thank you. Can I buy the socks,
  too? They're $11.99 a pair.
MRS. COOPER: How much is that altogether?
SALESPERSON: That's $111.99.
BETTY: I have the $11.99.

Complete the sentences.
- 1. Betty can't wear this pair of boots. They're ____ big. *too*
  2. ____ she wear that pair? ____, *they're too small.*
  3. She can wear one pair because they're just ____.
  4. But can she buy the boots? They're ____ expensive.
  5. Mrs. Cooper ____ Betty the money.
  6. ____ are the shoes and socks altogether?
  7. Now Betty is ____ happy.

C. Peter is in the men's department.

SALESPERSON: Can I help you?
PETER: Do you have any gray ties? It's a present for my father.
SALESPERSON: This department is full of ties. Yes, here's one.
PETER: Oh. How much is it?
SALESPERSON: Twelve seventy-five.
PETER: O.K. Do you have any blue and white shirts?
SALESPERSON: What size?
PETER: It's for my father, too. Not too big and not too small.
SALESPERSON: I see. Medium, then. This is a nice shirt.
PETER: Yes, that's the right size. How much is it?
SALESPERSON: Seventeen twenty-five.
PETER: That's so expensive. Well, it's all right. I have thirty-five
  dollars altogether.
SALESPERSON: Here's the sales slip. That's thirty dollars. Please,
  pay the bill to the cashier.
PETER: Can you put this shirt and tie in a box?
CASHIER: Sure. Here's your change.

Choose the correct answers.
- 1. Peter is in the *women's* / *men's* department. *men's*
  2. Peter is buying a shirt and *tie* / *socks.*
  3. The shirt is for Peter's *friend* / *father.*
  4. The shirt is *blue* / *green* and white.
  5. The cashier can put the tie and shirt in a *bag* / *box.*
  6. The shirt and tie are *forty* / *thirty* dollars.

=========== *Let's Talk* ===========

What's the temperature?
The temperature outside is 35°C (thirty-five degrees Celsius). It's very
hot outside. Discuss how you feel about going....

Are we going shopping?	*No, let's not. It's too hot.*
	It's thirty degrees outside.
Let's go swimming.	*It's twelve degrees outside.*
	It's too....
O.K. Let's go....	*Yes, let's. That's a good idea.*

A. Let's go to a restaurant.

It's getting late.
Mrs. Cooper, Peter, and
Betty are hungry.
They're in a restaurant
in the mall.   They're
giving their order to
the waiter.

MRS. COOPER: What's your soup today?
WAITER: We have vegetable soup or chicken soup.
MRS. COOPER: Let's see.   How about some chicken soup?
WAITER: Do you want coffee, tea, or milk?
MRS. COOPER: Oh, I can't decide.   Peter, do you want a hamburger?
PETER: What is there for dessert?
MRS. COOPER: Wait a minute, Peter.   First, order your dinner.
   Then think about dessert.
WAITER: Hot dogs are on special today.
PETER: Oh, now I can't decide.
WAITER: Miss, do you want the chicken soup, too?
BETTY: No, I don't.   Does the chicken dinner come with
   mashed potatoes or French fries?
WAITER: You can have one or the other.
BETTY: Now, I have to decide.   Then, I can order.

•MENU•

Soups
Chicken 1.25
Vegetable 1.25

Dinners
Steak 12.95
Chicken 9.75
Fish and Chips 6.85

Sandwiches
Hamburger, lettuce and tomato ... 3.50
Cheeseburger, lettuce and tomato ... 3.75

Today's Special
Hot dog with French fries ... 2.50

Beverages
Coffee, tea .... .50
juice, milk .... .75

Desserts
Ice cream 1.25
Pie 1.50

Choose the menu for the Coopers. List the prices. Then total the check.

Mrs. Cooper:		Peter:		Betty:	
Chicken soup	$1.25	_____	$_____	_____	$_____
_____	$_____	_____	$_____	_____	$_____
_____	$_____	_____	$_____	_____	$_____
_____	$_____	_____	$_____	_____	$_____
Total	$_____	Total	$_____	Total	$_____

Complete the sentences and answer the questions.

■ 1. Mrs. Cooper is ordering some chicken _____. *soup*
2. Betty has to decide. _____, she can order.
3. Peter is having _____. Then he's having _____.
4. Is Betty having French fries?   Is she having a beverage?
5. What's Mrs. Cooper having for dessert?
6. How much is Peter's check?
7. What is Betty's total?

Let's Talk

Here's your check.

You and your classmate are having lunch.
YOU: Can we have our check, please?
WAITRESS: Here you are.
YOU: Thank you.
CLASSMATE: How much is it?
YOU: Let's see. A cheeseburger is $3.75 and juice is $.75. That's
$4.50 altogether and $.70 for a tip. My check is $5.20. How much is
your check?
CLASSMATE: A...is...and....

Grammar: Items 1 and 3

Review

Ask and answer questions. Here are some examples.
What's Mrs. Cooper doing? Is she paying her check?
How much are the tires? , How much is the radio?

Vocabulary

Nouns: cashier, department, dimes, penny, quarters

Adverbs: too

Adjectives: expensive

Complete the sentences. Use the vocabulary above.
1. Alan has two _____. He has fifty cents.
2. Please pay the _____. She's standing over there.
3. Tom can't buy that guitar. It's _____ expensive.
4. Peter has a _____. He has one cent.
5. This shirt isn't too big. It's _____ right.
6. Betty has twenty cents. She has two _____.
7. These shoes are forty-nine dollars. They're very _____.
8. Do you have any records in this _____? *Yes, we do.*

Grammar

1. **Question word patterns**
   How much money do you have?

2. **Adjectives**
   These are *some* dimes on the table.
   No, there aren't *any* dimes.
   Are there *any* quarters?
   No, there aren't *any* quarters but there are *some* nickels.

3. **Adverbs**
   I want to buy that skirt.   It's *so* pretty.
                                       It's *very* pretty.
   I can't buy those boots.   They're *so* expensive.
                                       They're *too* expensive.

   PETER: I have to have a shirt — not too big and not too small.
   SALESPERSON: Medium *then*?
   PETER: Can I try on the shirt? *Then* I can decide.

4. **Verbs**
   Betty and Mrs. Cooper *are going* shopping.

5. **U.S. monetary units**

penny	— one cent	—	1¢
nickel	— five cents	—	5¢
dime	— ten cents	—	10¢
quarter	— twenty-five cents	—	25¢
half dollar	— fifty cents	—	50¢
dollar	— one hundred cents	—	$1.00

6. **Numbers**
   twenty-one, fifty-three

Test • Unit 15

15•1   Complete the sentences.

1. _____ is this blouse? _____ *twenty dollars.*
2. _____ those jeans? _____ *eighteen dollars.*
3. Are there _____ shoes in the closet? *Yes, _____.*
4. _____ coats in the window?
   No, _____ coats, but there are _____ jackets.

Write the words for these prices.
5. $97.00
6. $ 1.28
7. 59¢
8. $36.75

15•2   Complete the sentences.

1. Mrs. Cooper, Betty, and Peter are going _____ at the mall.
2. They _____ to buy some new clothes.
3. Betty is _____ on some boots.
4. She can't wear that pair. They're _____ small.
5. This pair is _____ right. But they're _____ expensive.
6. Mrs. Cooper is _____ Betty the money. Now Betty is _____ happy.
7. The shirt size is _____, not too big and not too small.
8. He has thirty-five dollars _____.

15•3   Read the story.

   Betty and Peter are so hungry. They're in a restaurant at the mall.
Peter is having a hamburger, French fries, and ice cream for dessert. Is
Betty having soup or hot dogs on special today? She has to decide first.
Then she can order.

Answer *That's right* **or** *That's wrong.*
1. Peter and Betty aren't very hungry.
2. Peter is having the hot dogs on special today.
3. Peter isn't having any beverage.
4. Betty has to order first.   Then she can decide.
5. Peter is having pie for dessert.

14•1 Make sentences plural with the word in italics.

1. There is one *dress* on the bed. _____ four _____ in the closet.
2. This is a new *blouse*. _____ some old _____ .
3. Here is a big *bus*. There _____ small _____ .
4. I have one *pair of* shoes and three _____ socks.
5. Betty has one *pair*. How many _____ do you have?
6. My *house* is small. Some _____ big.
7. This is a green *bush*. _____ some yellow _____ .
8. She has a long *nose*. They _____ short _____ .
9. One *cage* is on the shelf. Three _____ in the closet.
10. Let's carry the small *box*. Let's not carry the heavy _____ .

14•2 Complete the sentences. Use *this, these, that, those*.

1. Are _____ your records here?
2. _____ is Tom's book here.
3. Is _____ your pencil over there?
4. Are _____ Peter's friends across the street?

Complete the sentences.
5. Where _____ the jeans?
   One _____ *is on the chair. The* _____ *is on the floor.*
6. Whose dresses _____ they?
   One _____ *is Mary's and* _____ *dress is Elena's.*

Extra!

How many words can you find?

R	I	G	H	T	I	N	B	E	D
U	M	U	O	A	R	E	I	S	E
N	U	I	N	K	I	C	K	T	S
I	S	T	W	E	L	V	E	O	K
N	I	A	T	U	N	D	E	R	A
E	C	R	O	L	I	S	T	E	N

Key Sentences

Introduction

Tom has a bicycle and a radio. Where's the coat? It's on the bed. How many? What's this? It's a shoe. Yes, it is. No, it isn't. Is this a truck or a car?

UNIT ONE

How are you? What's that? Is this a pencil? Is this your book? You have a bicycle. Is this a short ruler? Where's the coat? What is it? She has five books. His name is Mr. Brown. He's a teacher. What's Mrs. Cooper doing? What are you doing? See you later.

UNIT TWO

This is the Cooper family. Is he Peter's father? Is she Betty's mother? What's your friend's name? This is Betty's friend. Her name is Helen. Are you Chinese? How old is Peter? Where is he from? How old are you? Who is it? Really? Is she writing? Welcome to Chicago! Call information. Ask for the number of a friend.

UNIT THREE

What's this? What's that? Where is it? It's on the floor. It's in the book. What's on the wall? It's big. What a lot of records! That's right. What a big family! Air mail postage, please.

UNIT FOUR

Can you see Peter? Yes, I can. No, he can't. Helen can see a lake. She can't see a cat. I can see a man, but I can't see a woman. What can you do? Mr. Cooper is behind Peter. Where's the curtain? Is the shoe under the bed or on the bed? Can you help me? Where's the bookcase?

UNIT FIVE

Betty is playing beachball. What's Mrs. Cooper doing? What's Peter doing now? What are you doing? She's looking out the window. I'm playing a record. She isn't looking at the flowers. Fill in the details. Wait a minute! Betty is sick. Please be quiet! What are the words?

UNIT SIX

How many cassettes can you see? He's recording a record. These aren't tables. Can't you see four people? Betty is visiting Elena now. Thank you for the gift. I'm counting everything. What are these? Are they tapes? How do you spell this?

UNIT SEVEN

Are these Tom's records? Where are Peter's shoes? Peter is in Tom's room. He's putting things on the shelf. What are they? Where are they? What is he doing? What are they doing? What am I doing? His room isn't neat. It's very messy. They're playing in Peter's room. Betty is in her room. Where is it going?

UNIT EIGHT

We're the Amoroso family. We're outside. Can you swim? Are you watching television? What can you do? It's our house. Are these my footballs? It's their car. Can you believe it? You're late, Peter. It is sitting in its cage. What are you doing? Excuse me. This isn't your package.

UNIT NINE	They're buying a record. Who's this? Let's go home now. What can we do tonight? They're practicing. Who's singing? What are they doing in the first picture? Who's where? Who are Alan and Roger? Who are they? Where are they? He can't. They can't. Here's the money. What's the occupation?
UNIT TEN	This is a shopping bag. Do you have my new magazine? What else do you have in your bag? I have a pencil, but I don't have an eraser. What do you have? Do they have your records? Peter, sit on the chair, please. Where are they going? Find it! Have you got a pen? What have you got in your bag? What a pretty house! Take a trip.
UNIT ELEVEN	It's here. It's over there. This is a car. That's a van. Where's my book? What are three things you can find in a bookstore? How many continents are there? He's swimming across the river. It's behind the bus. Play your radio after school. What's where?
UNIT TWELVE	What's wrong with Linda? Does she have a headache? Call an office. Carlos is feeling sad and Peter is, too. Peter doesn't have a cold. The Coopers don't have a van. They have a car. How do you feel? Carlos is sick, too. Dr. Jones is writing a textbook. Find out what's wrong.
UNIT THIRTEEN	Frank has to wash his hands. Do you have to take medicine? No, we don't. What do you have to do? Make and refuse invitations. Whose living room is this? It's a rainy day. Give directions. Can Peter go over to see Carlos? Peter can lend Carlos his records. Peter and Carlos are drawing. Where is the restroom?
UNIT FOURTEEN	Linda has two pairs of slippers. Whose shorts are they? Tom is packing his suitcase. Find the owner. Those are boots. The other pair is Tom's. How many pairs? What's going on? It's a surprise. What are you wearing?
UNIT FIFTEEN	Are there any jeans? How much are the jeans? Ask the salesperson the price of things. They are all going shopping. These boots are so pretty. Peter is in the men's department. What's the temperature? Let's go to a restaurant. Here's your check.

English Sounds

æ*	album, bag	o	open, home, so
e	ailment, airmail, pay	ɔ	all, long
ɛr	careful, chair	ɔɪ	boy
ɑ	are, father	ʊ	book
b	big, above, job	u	boot, school, shoe
tʃ	cheeseburger, picture, catch	aʊ	out, about, how
d	dog, shoulder, side	p	park, apple, stop
ɛ	enter, dress	r	red, erase, car
i	eat, feet, really	s	school, test, pants
f	feet, office, laugh	ʃ	shop, cashier, fish
g	go, degree, egg	t	take, stop, it
h	hat, aha	θ	thing, tooth
hw	what	ð	this, other
ɪ	eraser, fix	ʌ	under, cup
aɪ	idea, write, buy	ɜr	work
ɪr	ear, here	v	very, never, have
dʒ	job, beverage	w	want
k	cat, occupation, kick	j	yes, use
l	lend, milk, medical	z	zero, crazy
m	mother, classmate, drum	ʒ	garage
n	no, count, down	ə	about, careful, umbrella
ŋ	angry, running	ɚ	record, number
ɑ	want, volleyball		

---

* International Phonetic Alphabet

English Words Index

boy, 6   bɔɪ
bring, 126   brɪŋ
broken, 104   bro'kən
brother, 12   brʌð'ɚ
brown, 4   braun
building, 55   bɪl'dɪŋ
bus, 76   bʌs
bush, 22   buʃ
bus stop, 95   bʌs'-stap
but, 33   bʌt
buy, 82   baɪ
by, 7   baɪ

C

cage, 33   kedʒ
call, 17   kɔl
call up, 114   kɔ'ʌp
can, 32   kæn
can't, 32   kænt
car, 4   kɑr
card, 55   kɑrd
carrot, 92   kær'ət
carry, 106   kær'i
cash, 73   kæʃ
cashier, 145   kæ-ʃɪr'
cassette, 52   kæ-sɛt'
cat, ii   kæt
catch, 42   kætʃ
cent, 149   sɛnt
chair, i   tʃɛr
change, 93, 145   tʃendʒ
check, 73, 147   tʃɛk
cheeseburger, 147   tʃiz'bɜr'gɚ
chicken, 92   tʃɪk'ən
chin, 117   tʃɪn
class, 127   klæs
classmate, 3   klæs'met'
classroom, 95   klæs'rum'
clean, 7, 54   klin
clear up, 83   klɪr'ʌp
clerk, 27   klɜrk
clock, 52   klɑk
closet, ii   klɑz'ɪt
clothes, 66   kloz
coat, ii   kot
coffee, 7   kɔ'fi
cold, 114, 137   kold
color, 4   kʌl'ɚ
comb, 65   kom
come, 66   kʌm

come here, 17   kʌm-hɪr'
come on, 56   kʌm-ɑn'
comic book, 104   kɑm'ɪk-buk
compliment, 25   kɑm'plə-mənt
continent, 105   kɑn'tə-nənt
cook, 46   kuk
cooky, 92   kuk'i
corner, 95   kɔr'nər
correct, 107   kə-rɛkt'
count, 52   kaunt
country, 15   kʌn'tri
crazy about, 53   kre'zi-əbaut
cup, 124   kʌp
curtain, 35   kɜrt'n
customer, 56   kʌs'təm-ɚ

D

dad, 73   dæd
day, 124   de
decide, 146   dɪ-saɪd'
degree, 145   dᶻ-gri'
department, 144   dɪ-pɑrt'mənt
department store, 142
    dɪ-pɑrt'mənt-stɔr
desk, i   dɛsk
dessert, 146   dɪ-zɜrt'
detail, 45   dɪ-tel'
dime, 143   daɪm
dinner, 146   dɪn'ɚ
directions, 125   dɪ-rɛk'ʃənz
dirty, 26   dɜr'ti
do, 7   du
doctor, 113   dɑk'tɚ
doctor's orders, 126   dɑk'tɚz-ɔr'dɚz
dog, ii   dɔg
dollar, 143   dɑl'ɚ
door, 36   dɔr
down, 137   daun
draw, 45, 47   drɔ
dress, 132   drɛs
drink, 7   drɪŋk
drive, 73   draɪv
drugstore, 103   drʌg'stɔr'
drum, 52   drʌm

E

ear, 117   ɪr
eastern, 105   i'stɚn
easy, 76   i'zi
eat, 72   it

egg, 92 ɛg
elbow, 117 ɛl′bo
else, 93 ɛls
enter, 65 ɛn′tɚ
erase, 107 ɪ-res′
eraser, 2 ɪ-re′sɚ
evening, 83 iv′nɪŋ
everything, 56 ɛv′ri-θɪŋ′
exchange, 83 ɛks-tʃendʒ′
excuse, 77 ɛk-skjuz′
expensive, 55 ɛk-spɛn′sɪv
eye, 117 aɪ

F

family, 12 fæm′ə-li
famous, 15 fe′məs
father, 12 fɑ′ðɚ
favor, 35 fe′vɚ
feel, 114 fil
feet, 127 fit
female, 113 fi′mel′
fever, 112 fi′vɚ
finally, 83 faɪ′nə-li
find, 95 faɪnd
fine, thank you, 2 faɪn-θæŋk-ju
fine, thanks, 27 faɪn-θæŋks
finger, 117 fɪŋ′gɚ
first to fifth, 85 fɜrst-tu-fɪfθ
fish and chips, 147 fɪʃ-ənd-tʃɪps
fix, 64 fɪks
floor, 5 flɔr
floor plan, 107 flɔr′plæn
flower, 44 flaʊ′ɚ
flu, 114 flu
foot, 117 fʊt
football, 72 fʊt′bɔl′
for, 84 fɔr
found, 33 faʊnd
French fries, 146 frɛntʃ′fraɪz
friend, 3 frɛnd
from, 14 frʌm
front, 23 frʌnt
full of, 145 fʊl-ʌv
funny, 124 fʌn′i

G

game, 114 gem
garage, 84 gə-rɑʒ′
garden, 44 gɑrd′n
gardener, 122 gɑrd′nɚ

get home, 76 gɛt-hom
get to school, 76 gɛt-tu-skul
gift, 27 gɪft
girl, 6 gɜrl
give, 97 gɪv
gladly, 137 glæd′li
glasses, 134 glæ′sɛz
glove, 132 glʌv
go, 64 go
good, 83 gʊd
good afternoon, 3 gʊd-æf′tɚ-nun′
good-by, 7 gʊd′baɪ′
good morning, 2 gʊd-mɔr′nɪŋ
go on, 136 go-ɑn′
gray, 145 gre
great, 115 gret
green, 4 grin
guitar, ii gɪ-tɑr′

H

hair, 65 hɛr
half dollar, 149 hæf-dɑl′ɚ
hall, 95 hɔl
hamburger, 46 hæm′bɜr′gɚ
hand, 117 hænd
happy, 114 hæp′i
has, 4 hæz
hat, 4 hæt
have, 4 hæv
have a good time, 72
  hæv-ə-gʊd-taɪm
he, 4 hi
head, 117 hɛd
headache, 112 hɛd′ek′
headphone, 57 hɛd′fon′
hear, 66 hɪr
heavy, 106 hɛv′i
hello, 3 hɛ-lo′
help, 35 hɛlp
hemisphere, 105 hɛm′ə-sfɪr′
her, 6 hɜr
here, 83 hɪr
hey, 17 he
hi, 2 haɪ
his, 6 hɪs
hold, 43 hold
home, 107 hom
homework, 35 hom′wɜrk′
hot dog, 146 hɑt′dɔg
hospital, 112 hɑs′pə-təl

house, 32 haʊs
how are you, 2 haʊ-ɑr-ju
how many, iv haʊ-mɛn'i
how much, 143 haʊ-mʌtʃ
how old are you?, 14
  haʊ-old-ɑr-ju
hungry, 92 hʌŋ'gri

I
I, 2, 6 aɪ
ice cream, 72 aɪs'krim
idea, 82 aɪ-di'ə
ill, 114 ɪl
in, iii ɪn
information, 17 ɪn'fɚ-me'ʃən
in front of, 34 ɪn-frʌnt'ʌv
initials, 17 ɪ-nɪʃ'əlz
inside, 73 ɪn-saɪd'
instruments, 84 ɪn'strə-mənts
interesting, 55 ɪn'trɪ-stɪŋ
into, 64 ɪn'tu
invitation, 123 ɪn'və-te'ʃən
invite, 123 ɪn-vaɪt'
is, iii, vi, 3 ɪz
island, 22 aɪ'lənd
it, iii, vi, 3 ɪt
its, 77 ɪts

J
jacket, 102 dʒæk'ɪt
jeans, 133 dʒinz
job, 87 dʒɑb
jog, 42 dʒɑg
juice, 147 dʒus
jump, 66 dʒʌmp
just right, 144 dʒʌst-raɪt

K
key, i ki
kick, 16 kɪk
kidding, 75 kɪd'ɪŋ
kitchen, 92 kɪtʃ'ən
kite, 24 kaɪt
knee, 117 ni

L
lake, 32 lek
lamp, 33 læmp
last, 85 læst
late, 76 let

laugh, 46 læf
learn, 125 lɜrn
leave, 65 liv
leg, 112 lɛg
lend, 127 lɛnd
letter, 7 lɛt'ɚ
lie, 44 laɪ
listen, 64 lɪs'ən
living room, 97 lɪv'ɪŋ-rum
location, 107 lo-ke'ʃən
long, 4 lɔŋ
look, 23 lʊk
lunch, 113 lʌntʃ

M
magazine, 92 mæg'ə-zin'
mail, 27 mel
make, 85 mek
male, 113 mel
man, 15 mæn
many, 52 mɛn'i
map, 24 mæp
married, 113 mær'id
mashed, 146 mæʃt
match, 67 mætʃ
measles, 114 mi'zəlz
medical, 113 mɛd'ɪ-kəl
medicine, 116 mɛd'ə-sən
medium, 145 mi'di-əm
men, 124 mɛn
menu, 147 mɛn'ju
mess, 62 mɛs
messy, 66 mɛs'i
microphone, 67 maɪ'krə-fon'
middle, 53 mɪd'l
milk, 146 mɪlk
minute, 46 mɪn'ɪt
Miss, 146 mɪs
mistakes, 57 mɪ-steks'
mom, 73 mɑm
money, 87 mʌn'i
mother, 12 mʌð'ɚ
motorcycle, 22 mo'tɚ-saɪ'kəl
mouse, 33 maʊs
mouth, 116 maʊθ
Mr., 2 mɪs'tɚ
Mrs., 7 mɪs'ɪz
Ms., 113 mɪz
music, 53 mju'zɪk
musician, 86 mju-zɪʃ'ən

my, 2   maɪ

N

nail, 117   nel
name, 2   nem
neat, 66   nit
necktie, 132   nɛk′taɪ′
never, 76   nɛv′ɚ
new, 25   nu
newspaper, 77   nuz′pe′pɚ
nice, 3   naɪs
nickel, 143   nɪk′əl
no, vi   no
noise, 87   nɔɪz
northern, 105   nɔr′ðɚn
nose, 117   noz
notebook, 94   not′bʊk′
not, 3   nɑt
not bad, 3   nɑt-bæd
now, 43   naʊ
number, iv   nʌm′bɚ
    1 to 12,iv
    13 to 20, 14
    21 to 101, 143

O

object, 5   ɑb′dʒɛkt
occupation, 87   ɑk′jə-pe′ʃən
ocean, 43   o′ʃən
of, 65   ʌv
of course, 97   ʌv-kɔrs′
office, 113   ɔ′fɪs
oh, 17   o
O.K., 7   o-ke′
old, 75   old
on, iii, 66   ɑn
one, 132   wʌn
on time, 77   ɑn-taɪm
onto, 66   ɑn′tu′
open, 36   o′pən
operator, 17   ɑp′ə-re′tɚ
or, vi   ɔr
orange, 2, 4   ɔr′ɪndʒ
organ, 84   ɔr′gən
other, 134   ʌð′ɚ
our, 74   aʊr
out, 44   aʊt
out of, 65   aʊt-ʌv
outside, 73   aʊt-saɪd′
over there, 102   o′vɚ-ðɛr

owner, 133   on′ɚ

P

pack, 133   pæk
package, 77   pæk′ɪdʒ
pair, 132   pɛr
pants, 134   pænts
park, 72   pɑrk
party, 133   pɑr′ti
patient, 112   pe′ʃənt
pay, 145   pe
pen, i   pɛn
pencil, i   pɛn′səl
penny, 143   pɛn′i
people, 55   pi′pəl
person, 15   pɜr′sən
photograph, 85   fo′tə-græf′
piano, 52   pi-æn′o
picture, 23   pɪk′tʃɚ
pie, 147   paɪ
play, 17   ple
please, 27   pliz
pole, 105   pol
porch, 86   pɔrtʃ
possession, 95   pə-zɛʃ′ən
postage, 27   po′stɪdʒ
post office, 27   post-ɔ′fɪs
poster, 25   po′stɚ
potato, 146   pə-te′to
practice, 84   præk′tɪs
present, 82   prɜz′ənt
pretty, 55   prɪt′i
price, 142   praɪs
purse, ii   pɜrs
put, 62   pʊt
put on, 136   pʊt-ɑn

Q

quarter, 143   kwɔr′tɚ

R

radio, ii   re′di-o
rain, 83   ren
raincoat, 124   ren′kot′
rainy, 124   re′ni
read, 7   rid
really, 16   ri′ə-li′
receive, 127   rɪ-siv′
record, ii   rɛk′ɚd
record, 53   rɪ-kɔr′d

tape, 57 tep
tape recorder, 53 tep-rı-kɔr′dɚ
tea, 146 ti
teach, 127 titʃ
teacher, 6 ti′tʃɚ
teeth, 127 tiθ
telephone, i tɛl′ə-fon
telephone call, 126 tɛl′ə-fon-kɔl
television, 73 tɛl′ə-vɪʒ′ən
temperature, 112 tɛm′pɚ-ətʃur
tennis, 124 tɛn′ıs
tennis racket, 124 tɛn′ıs-ræk′ıt
terrible, 87 tɛr′ə-bəl
test, 116 tɛst
textbook, 104 tɛkst′buk′
thanks, 16 θæŋks
thank you, 2 θæŋk′ju
that, 2, 103 ðæt
that's a good idea, 82
  ðæts-ə-gud-aı-di′ə
that's right, 26 ðæts-raıt
the, iii ðə
their, 75 ðɛr
then, 145 ðɛn
there, 102 ðɛr
these, 54 ðiz
they, 57 ðe
thing, 55 θıŋ
think about, 146 θıŋk-ə-baut
this, vi ðıs
those, 134 ðoz
throat, 112 θrot
throw, 45 θro
thumb, 117 θʌm
thunder, 87 θʌn′dɚ
tie, 145 taı
tip, 147 tıp
tire, 102 taır
to, 43 tu
today, 87 tə-de′
together, 64 tə-gɛð′ɚ
tomato, 147 tə-me′to
tomorrow, 116 tə-mɔr′o
tonight, 83 tə-naıt′
too, 12, 114 tu
tooth, 127 tuθ
top, 23 tap
total, 147 tot′l
touch, 64 tʌtʃ
tree, 13 tri

trip, 97 trıp
truck, vi trʌk
try on, 144 traı-an
turntable, 57 tɚrn te′bəl
TV, 34 tivi′

U
umbrella, 2 ʌm-brɛl′ə
under, iii ʌn′dɚ
unusual, 75 ʌn′ju′ʒu-əl
use, iv juz

V
van, 102 væn
vegetable, 93 vɛdʒ′tə-bəl
very, 66 vɛr′i
vest, 134 vɛst
visit, 55 vız′ıt
visitor, 127 vız′ə-tɚ
vocabulary, iv vo-kæb′jə-lɛr′i
volleyball, 42 val′i-bɔl

W
wait, 46 wet
wait a minute, 46 wet-ə-mın′ıt
waiter, 145 we′tɚ
waitress, 147 we′trıs
walk, 43 wɔk
wall, 24 wɔl
want, 146 want
wash, 137 waʃ
washing, 122 waʃ′ıŋ
washing machine, 137
  waʃ′ıŋ-mə-ʃin
watch, i, 64 watʃ
we, 72 wi
wear, 134 wɛr
weather, 83 wɛð′ɚ
welcome, 17 wɛl′kəm
welcome to, 17
  wɛl′kəm-tu
well, 87 wɛl
western, 105 wɛs′tɚn
what, vi, 7 hwat
what a, 25 hwat-ə
what a lot of, 25 hwat-ə-lat-ʌv
what's wrong, 112 hwats-rɔŋ
where, iii hwɛr
white, 4 hwaıt
who, 82 hwu

(one hundred sixty-one) **161**

who's, whose, 124 hwuz
window, ii wɪn'do
window-shop, 142 wɪn'do-ʃɑp
windowsill, 104 wɪn'do-sɪl'
windy, 136 wɪn'di
wire, 64 waɪr
with, 42 wɪθ
woman, 15 wʊm'ən
women, 124 wɪm'ən
work, 56 wɝk
workbook, 104 wɝk'bʊk'
worry, 116 wɝ'i

wow, 55 waʊ
wrist, 117 rɪst
write, 7 raɪt
wrong, 112 rɑŋ

Y
yard, 24 jɑrd
year, 12 jɪr
yellow, 4 jɛl'o
yes, vi jɛs
you, 2, 72 ju
your, 2, 74 jʊr

Grammar Index

The number after each category indicates the page on which a new item or pattern first appears.

ABCDEFGHIJ-H-8210